# BANKERS, STATESMEN
# AND ECONOMISTS

# BANKERS, STATESMEN AND ECONOMISTS

BY

PAUL EINZIG, 1897 –

*Essay Index Reprint Series*

*Originally published by:*

MACMILLAN AND CO., LIMITED

BOOKS FOR LIBRARIES PRESS, INC.

FREEPORT, NEW YORK

First Published 1935
Reprinted 1967

LIBRARY OF CONGRESS CATALOG CARD NUMBER:
67-30185

PRINTED IN THE UNITED STATES OF AMERICA

# PREFACE

THE publication of a volume of essays is a new departure for the author. In deciding upon it, he followed the suggestion of several friends, reinforced by encouragement from readers of his various books and articles. They pointed out that there were many subjects which, while not sufficiently broad to occupy a whole book, could and should be dealt with by independent essays within the covers of a single volume.

Accordingly, the author embarked upon the difficult task of selecting from among his various articles and lectures those which were suitable for reproduction in a less ephemeral form. Since, however, he has usually dealt with essentially topical problems, the majority of the articles and lectures had to be ruled out because in the meantime the march of events had rendered them obsolete. It was tempting in many cases to reproduce such obsolete material in order to be able to point out triumphantly that events had developed to a large extent in the directions forecast by the author. He resisted this temptation, not for considerations of false modesty, but because he believes that from the point of view of general readers such an attitude of "I told you so" must appear somewhat irritating. Moreover, they have every right to suspect authors who indulge in that attitude of having picked out only those forecasts which have proved to be right, wisely

v

omitting those which have proved wrong. For these reasons, the author decided to bring all his topical material up to date, and instead of presenting his readers with his views of, say, March 1933 or October 1934, to present them with his views of September 1935.

Accordingly, he has revised to a greater or less extent most of the articles that have appeared in various newspapers and magazines. There are, however, a few essays in this volume the subjects of which are not quite so topical as the rest, and which the author consequently has left unchanged in their original form. These essays include the summary of a lecture he delivered before the Cornhill Club in January 1935 under the title of "Bankers and Deflation". Two other essays, "Bankers and Stabilisation" and "Bankers and Inflation", were published in *The Banker*. The essay on "Central Banks and Treasuries" was published by *Barrons Weekly*. "Changes in the Practice and Technique of Central Banking" and "The Future of the Bank for International Settlements" were published in the Central Banking supplement of *Indian Finance*. "Germany's Economic Recovery" and "France's Crisis" are reprinted from *Current History* of New York. "The Financial Triangle" appeared in the Italian monthly magazine *Rassegna di Politica Internazionale*. The author would like to thank the Editors of these publications for their permission to reprint these essays.

By far the larger part of the volume contains entirely original material. Most important amongst them is, in the author's opinion, "The Case against Stabilisation". The author has viewed with growing uneasiness the conversion of some radical economists, such as Sir Arthur Salter, Mr J. M. Keynes, and Mr Hubert Henderson, in favour of some form of immediate stabilisation. While he himself is for our eventual return to some kind of gold standard, he considers it of vital importance that this step should not be taken prematurely. He feels equally strongly against falling into the ingenious traps laid by orthodox adherents of stabilisation, who, realising that for the present a return to the gold standard is out of the question, would like to lure Great Britain and other countries into stabilisation by inducing them to adopt some kind of informal *de facto* stability. The first essay in this volume endeavours to warn against falling into such traps.

Four other original essays deal with some of the most discussed personalities of contemporary history. "President Roosevelt through European Eyes" endeavours to vindicate the unorthodox policy pursued in the United States since 1933 at a time when it is fashionable to talk about the failure of that policy and its inaugurator. The author does not seek to minimise the mistakes committed—in fact, he concludes that President Roosevelt has all along been doing the right thing in the wrong way. He holds the view, however, that President Roosevelt will in the long run produce a more profound impression upon the evolution of Europe than any of his fellow-countrymen before him.

The other extreme is represented by Mr Montagu Norman, whose orthodox policy is criticised in an essay in which the author has had to confess to having changed his views considerably on his subject. Under the influence of the events of the last few years, the author, together with many others, has become converted to the necessity of pursuing ·a more radical monetary policy than was followed before the crisis. He arrived at this conclusion under the weight of unmistakable facts showing that the countries which have to some degree departed from orthodoxy have to a large extent recovered from the depression, while the countries whose monetary policy has continued to be ruled by orthodox doctrinairism have been drifting from bad to worse. One of Mr Montagu Norman's great faults is that he has failed to learn the lesson of the last few years. While the author admires him as a remarkable example of a remarkable type, and pays tribute to his character, he points out at the same time the dangerous consequences of Mr Norman's policy.

In contrast to Mr Norman, M. Van Zeeland is presented as the type of banker-statesman who understands the change of times and is able to discard traditionalism. The services he has rendered to his country, and by giving an example to the world in general, have not received adequate appreciation either in Belgium or abroad. In his essay the author seeks to pay him a long-overdue and well-deserved tribute.

"Signor Mussolini's Dilemma" analyses the conflict between the Duce's unorthodox economic policy and his extremely orthodox monetary policy, and the conflict between his desire for colonial expansion and his desire to defend the lira. When part of the present essay appeared in a series of articles in *The Financial News* in December 1934, it was followed by some violent personal attacks on the author in the Italian Press. During the past three years the author has perhaps written more in favour of the economic aspects of Italian Fascism than any other human being, but this fact did not safeguard him from being attacked by the Italian Press—which, as is well known, is under the strict control of the Minister of Propaganda—the moment he permitted himself some friendly criticism of one particular aspect of Signor Mussolini's policy. Nothing short of blind admiration satisfies the Great.

A brief essay examines the relation between the operations of the Exchange Equalisation Account and the changes in the amount of foreign balances in London. Another brief essay analyses the latest type of monetary policy, that of "consistent deflation". A somewhat longer essay deals with recent developments in the London gold market.

Finally, there are two essays, one of which is a metaphysical *jeu d'esprit* dealing with the question of whether the depression that began in 1929 can be called a "great" depression or merely a "big" depression. The other contains a practical suggestion as to how to end the crisis. It is the first time that the author has proposed a "patent medicine", and as he points out in his essay on "The Way Out", he is entitled for this reason to lenient treatment under the First Offenders' Act.

It goes without saying that it was impossible to deal in full detail with the various subjects discussed in the essays published in this volume. For those who are interested in the subjects, and in the author's point of view on those subjects, his earlier books provide much more detailed material. Those interested in the essays on monetary policy will find them discussed in fuller detail in *World Finance since 1914*, *The Future of Gold*, and *The Sterling-Dollar-Franc Tangle*. The essays on "Mr Montagu Norman's Policy", "Central Banks and Treasuries", and "Changes in Central Bank Technique and Practice" revise the author's views on Central Banking, as expressed in his book *Montagu Norman : A Study in Financial Statesmanship* and *The Bank for International Settlements*. The latter book is also brought up to date by the essay on "The Future of the Bank for International Settlements". Those interested in the essay on "The London Gold Market" will find fuller details in the author's books on *The Future of Gold* and *International Gold Movements*, while the essay on "Foreign Sterling Balances" deals with one aspect of the vast subject covered by the author's book on *Exchange Control*. "Signor Mussolini's Dilemma" is a sequel to the author's book *The Economic Foundations of Fascism*, although this essay, like all the other essays, is intelligible to those who have not read the corresponding book and have no intention of doing so. "Germany's Economic Recovery" revises *Germany's Default : The Economics of Hitlerism*, while "France's Crisis" brings up to date the author's book bearing the same title.

Presumably the reader may find this volume of essays rather a "mixed bag". Yet though the essays may differ in quantity, quality, and in the nature of their material, the reader will doubtless recognise that they are all inspired by the same spirit of revolt against the conventional teachings of the successors of classical economists who, in the author's opinion, have failed to realise that changed conditions necessitate a revision of outlook. Readers may be shocked by the author's radicalism in matters of monetary policy, by his attitude towards debts, independent central banking, etc. But even those who strongly disapprove of his point of view may find it beneficial to re-examine the new trend of economic thought which is unmistakably gaining ground throughout the world at the present juncture. Bankers, statesmen, and economists can no longer afford to ignore the new world trend. The common object of this collection of essays is to judge them according to whether or not they have realised the trend of evolution.

P. E.

THE WHITE COTTAGE
  SOUTH BOLTON GARDENS
    LONDON, S.W., *September* 1935

# CONTENTS

xiii

# THE CASE AGAINST STABILISATION

## (1) A "STABILISATION OFFENSIVE"

THE suspension of the gold standard in Great Britain in September 1931 divided expert opinion in Great Britain into three camps. The orthodox school demanded that sterling should be re-stabilised immediately. The extreme radical school declared that we should never again return to the gold standard. Between these two extremes there was a moderate school of thought which, while favouring an eventual return to the gold standard, was opposed to premature stabilisation. For nearly four years a lively controversy has been going on between the three camps. In the course of this controversy, the moderate and radical schools joined forces against the orthodox school. Although they disagreed with each other as to the ultimate end of British policy, for the time being this question was regarded as a matter of academic importance. Their interest to oppose stabilisation, in the near future at any rate, was identical. Their aim consisted largely in maintaining the existing *status quo*. They were, therefore, on the defensive, while the orthodox school took the offensive—a strange reversal of the traditional rôles of orthodoxy and radicalism.

During the last few months the orthodox school has intensified its "stabilisation offensive". To some extent this has been due to the comparative stability of sterling since the beginning of 1935, which appeared to have improved the chances of some form

1

of stabilisation. The increasing unwillingness of the Washington Administration to avail itself of its right to devalue the dollar further has also encouraged the stabilisation party to renew its efforts. There has been indeed for some months a real barrage of demands for immediate and unconditional stabilisation.

The main strongholds of the stabilisation movement are the Bank of England, the London School of Economics, and the Sound Currency Association. The Bank of England is known from the very outset to have been in favour of an early re-stabilisation. Its opposition to the Treasury's contrary policy, although it has taken place behind the scenes, has been an open secret. It would be contrary to the traditions of the Bank of England to express views criticising the Government's policy, but implied and indirect criticism has been directed against it none the less by means of the periodical statements issued by the Board of Directors of the Bank for International Settlements, which, as is well known, includes Mr Montagu Norman and Sir Otto Niemeyer. Although Mr Montagu Norman's influence on the Treasury is nothing like as great as before the crisis, his strong personality has remained a factor to be reckoned with.

The London School of Economics has always been the spearhead in the academic field of the movement in favour of an orthodox monetary policy. It will be remembered that soon after the war Professor Cannan went so far in his zeal as to start a legal action against the Treasury for profiteering on the ground that it was selling bits of paper worth a fraction of a farthing for ten shillings or a pound. It is in accordance with the traditions of that school that it should provide the theoretical ammunition for the fight in favour of immediate stabilisation. Professor Hayek, inspired by a dislike for any departure from orthodoxy that originated during the disastrous inflationary period in Austria, has infused fresh blood into the school. With Professors Gregory and Robbins, he has constituted a trio which is a factor of importance in the controversy.

## (2) BANKERS' ATTITUDE

The Sound Currency Association was for years moribund; for with the stabilisation of sterling at its pre-war parity in 1925 it achieved its main object. Although its various supporters never ceased to agitate between 1921 and 1931 in favour of reducing the fiduciary issue, they stirred up but little interest. The Association was revived recently by its originator, Mr D. M. Mason, M.P., who never misses an opportunity in the House of Commons of impressing upon the Government the necessity for immediate stabilisation. The fact that the chairman of one of the Big Five has joined the Association shows that it does not lack support in influential banking circles. Another organisation which works in the same direction but which is less known is the "Friends of Economy" movement; it suffered a severe reverse through the disappearance of *The Independent*, a weekly paper established by Sir Ernest Benn for the purpose of supporting orthodox ideas in the sphere of monetary, financial, and economic policy.

In addition to the systematic efforts of these institutions, the movement in favour of stabilisation receives support from time to time from various bankers and business men in the form of public statements urging an immediate return to gold. The frequency of such statements at shareholders' meetings or at various City banquets has conveyed the impression that opinion in the City is practically unanimous and in favour of immediate stabilisation. This is not the case. A large proportion of leading bankers and City men are opposed to it, but they are reluctant to express their opinion in public. On the other hand, those in favour of the orthodox policy never miss an opportunity for doing so. In some cases, at any rate, an emphatic declaration made at a shareholders' meeting urging the necessity of immediate stabilisation has served the useful purpose of diverting attention from the weak points of the balance-sheets. Since the majority of City editors are inclined to share these views, the financiers concerned were certain to secure for themselves a favourable Press on the basis of their "sound" views, even though there was nothing else sound in their annual reports. It never occurs to anyone to ask whether these financiers, having mismanaged the affairs of their own companies, are qualified to advise the Government and the public on the management of the affairs of the country.

Among politicians the idea of immediate stabilisation has received frequent support, especially on the part of the Liberal opposition, though the Labour opposition has been definitely against it. On the rare occasions when the Government's monetary policy has been put to the vote in the House of Commons there has invariably been a large majority in favour of it.

### (3) DEGREES OF STABILISATION

Those in favour of immediate stabilisation are by no means unanimous as to the degree and nature of stabilisation. Their proposals may be summarised as follows:

1. The restoration of the full automatic gold standard as it worked before the war.
2. The restoration of a gold standard of which the automatic working should be tempered by management in the form of open market operations, international co-operation, etc., such as existed after 1925.
3. The establishment of a fully managed gold standard, *i.e.* a managed currency with gold backing.
4. Stabilisation of sterling in relation to gold without restoring its convertibility.
5. Stabilisation of sterling in relation to gold with a fairly wide margin of fluctuation.
6. Stabilisation of sterling on the understanding that its parity might be changed in case of adverse pressure.
7. *De facto* stabilisation of sterling for experimental purposes.

We do not propose to examine in detail these various proposals. The difference between them is of vital importance when it comes to deciding what system is to be adopted eventually, but from the point of view of the immediate problem the difference between them is merely one of degree. In every case, the adoption of the proposal would mean a change in the monetary policy of the Government, which at present retains an absolutely free hand to alter the gold value of sterling. Even if only experimental pre-stabilisation were adopted it would tend to tie the Government's hands, for once the exchange was fixed for any length of time influences working in favour of retaining it at that level permanently would be bound to increase considerably. Indeed, in many cases, the adherents of full stabilisation pretend to be satisfied as a first step with provisional *de facto* stabilisation in the hope that by this display of moderation they may lure their opponents into a compromise. It is the first step that is difficult. Once the Government had agreed to adopt a policy of stabilisation, however provisional and informal, it would be difficult to return to the policy of a free hand.

In addition to the pressure brought to bear upon the British Government from various British quarters, a regular stabilisation offensive is raging against this country from abroad. Whenever some international economic, financial, or commercial organisation meets it never misses an opportunity to declare itself in favour of immediate stabilisation. Resolutions to that effect have come to be regarded as indispensable at meetings of the Bank for International Settlements, the International Chamber of Commerce, various committees and sub-committees of the League of Nations, and other official, semi-official, or private conferences. In the Press of the Gold Bloc countries, Great Britain is presented as the villain of the piece, whose unwillingness to stabilise at once is the main obstacle—indeed the only obstacle—to world-wide recovery, peace, and prosperity and everlasting happiness. Leading articles in continental newspapers advise, request, implore, and demand that sterling shall be stabilised forthwith.

What is more, even foreign statesmen and Central Bankers holding official positions consider it their right and duty to tell the British Government what it ought to do about British monetary policy. If a member of the British Government were to state his views that France, Holland, and Switzerland ought to devalue there would be an outburst of indignation in the Press of those countries and the British statesman would be sternly rebuked for his unwarranted interference with the monetary policy of other countries. Indeed, even if private individuals and privately owned newspapers in Great Britain venture to express the opinion that it is to the interest of the Gold Bloc to devalue, the Press of the countries concerned protests emphatically against such outside interference. This does not, however, prevent these countries from declaring officially that sterling should be stabilised, although this constitutes quite as much interference with the monetary affairs of another country as the advice given to the Gold Bloc to devalue.

### (4) ARGUMENTS FOR STABILISATION

The stabilisation offensive is directed against sterling from a variety of quarters, British and foreign. The weapons and projectiles used in the attack also vary immensely. Volumes could be written—indeed volumes are being written—about the arguments in favour of immediate stabilisation. In the present article we propose to confine ourselves to dealing only with the most popular of the arguments put forward by the adherents of the immediate stabilisation of sterling. These arguments can be summarised as follows:

1. It would bring about an all-round stabilisation of currencies and obviate the necessity for the Gold Bloc to devalue.
2. It would be followed by a general rise in the world price-level which would reduce the real

burden of national and international indebtedness.

3. It would lead to a restoration of confidence resulting in a world-wide recovery of trade.

4. It would lead to the elimination of the various restrictions on foreign trade and exchanges and would reduce Government intervention in general.

5. It would lead to higher interest rates, thereby checking the tendency towards over-speculation.

6. It would eliminate the danger of uncontrolled inflation that is associated with inconvertible currencies.

7. From a purely British point of view it would retain for sterling the advantages of undervaluation in relation to the currencies of the Gold Bloc and its satellites.

These and many other arguments have been repeated innumerable times by the adherents of immediate stabilisation. Let us see how far they can stand critical examination.

In the first place, it is highly doubtful whether the willingness of the British Government to stabilise sterling at present would in itself be sufficient to bring about world-wide stabilisation. Notwithstanding recent statements by Mr Morgenthau, the attitude of the United States in this respect is open to doubt. It is true that Mr Morgenthau has emphasised the willingness of the United States to stabilise immediately, but then he was perfectly safe in doing so, since he knew that his bluff would not be called. In the face of a strong Radical opposition, President Roosevelt can hardly afford to adopt an orthodox monetary policy before the presidential election of 1936. Even if he were to agree to stabilise the dollar definitely at its present level, there would remain the possibility that for internal political considerations he might have to change his policy during 1936. Nor is it certain that Japan would follow the British example and stabilise the yen. Indeed, should her ambitious policy in China materialise, it would become impossible for her to stabilise for some time to come. Nor would Germany be likely to relinquish the advantages of her elastic blocked currencies. As for Italy, the prospects of an Abyssinian war are in themselves sufficient to rule out the possibility of a stabilisation of the lira in the near future.

It is thus evident that the willingness of Great Britain to stabilise would not in itself be sufficient to restore international stability. Nor would it be sufficient to save the currencies of the Gold Bloc from devaluation. Given that at their present level they are out of equilibrium with sterling, the dollar, etc., they would remain vulnerable even after the stabilisation of those currencies. Their internal and international position would inevitably deteriorate and their eventual collapse would be a mere question of time. A sharp rise in the world price-level or a fundamental recovery of trade would conceivably save the gold currencies, but as we shall see later the chances are overwhelmingly against such developments. In the course of a year or two after the stabilisation of sterling we should witness, therefore, a depreciation or devaluation of the gold currencies which would once more upset international stability.

Doubtless this source of danger can be removed if the stabilisation of sterling is preceded by or is made

to coincide with a devaluation of the gold currencies
to a level that would secure a reasonable degree of
equilibrium. There remains, however, the question of
whether at its present level sterling is not overvalued
by comparison with the dollar, and whether its technical position after stabilisation would be strong enough
to safeguard it against another depreciation. If the
currencies were stabilised in circumstances that
secured for the United States a perpetual huge export
surplus and which resulted in a flow of gold to the
United States on a large scale, sterling would be exposed to the danger of having its gold reserve depleted
once more. This danger is all the greater as, in spite of
the increase of the British gold reserve through purchases by the Bank of England and the Exchange
Equalisation Account during the last few years, its
amount is still highly inadequate. Unless and until the
British authorities succeed in accumulating a gold
reserve far in excess of London's foreign short-term
indebtedness, sterling will remain vulnerable. There is
no reason to suppose, therefore, that in the existing
circumstances the stabilisation of sterling would lead
to lasting international monetary stability. The argument in favour of immediate stabilisation based on
that assumption is untenable.

## (5) STABILISATION AND WORLD PRICES

Another argument used by those supporting immediate stabilisation is that it would lead to a substantial rise in the world level of prices and would,
therefore, tend to eliminate various disequilibria both
internal and international. This argument is based on
certain assumptions. One is that the revival of confid-

ence in the stability of currencies would in itself produce psychological influences tending to raise commodity prices. Another assumption is that the revaluation of various gold reserves that would follow the stabilisation of currencies on lower parities would create possibilities of credit expansion that would lead to a rise in commodity prices. We have seen above that the first of these assumptions is not correct, since stabilisation in the existing conditions is not likely to inspire confidence in permanent stability. In any case, with industries working only to the extent of a small percentage of their capacity, and with agriculture, mining, etc., subject to artificial restrictions, the chances are that should stabilisation lead to a revival of confidence it would express itself in an increase of production rather than in an increase of prices. Useful as this would be, it would not contribute materially to the disappearance of the disequilibrium between price-levels in various countries, nor would it go very far towards the reduction of the real burden of indebtedness.

As for the possibilities of credit expansion following upon stabilisation, they would depend upon the extent to which the currencies were eventually devalued. On the basis of the existing level of sterling there would doubtless be a fair margin, though it would be a mistake to exaggerate it. It is certain that after stabilisation every Central Bank would endeavour to maintain a much higher reserve ratio than it did before the crisis. On the basis of a devaluation of about 40 per cent, this policy would leave only a relatively moderate margin for further expansion. Moreover, in the existing situation the policy pursued by Central Banks after stabilisation would not be one of expansion. The

adherents of immediate stabilisation are fully aware
of this, since they themselves admit that stabilisation
will be accompanied by higher money rates. Indeed,
in accordance with the time-honoured orthodox principle, a currency can only remain stable if it is being
kept scarce. Throughout post-war history, stabilisation was always followed by a period of money scarcity,
and there is no reason to suppose that it would be
otherwise if we stabilised under existing circumstances.

It would, therefore, be idle to expect a rise in commodity prices to follow upon international monetary
stabilisation. Indeed, the chances are that stabilisation
would be followed by an all-round revival of orthodoxy,
and that even in the United States it would damp the
inflationary tendencies of the official policy. As for the
countries of the Gold Bloc, they would have to deflate
in order to restore equilibrium. Their deflationary effort,
provided that it did not coincide with inflationary
expansion in other countries, would tend to depress
world prices in general. Thus, the balance of probability is if anything in favour of a fall in world prices
rather than a rise. Even if the gold countries were to
devalue prior to stabilisation, the best that could be
hoped for would be the absence of a fall in commodity
prices.

Another argument in favour of immediate stabilisation maintains that it would lead to a world-wide
recovery in trade as a result of the restoration of
confidence. Professor Rist in a recent article in *Lloyds
Bank Review* declared that a return to the gold standard would be followed by a decline of unemployment
all over the world through a revival of trade. In
this respect it is necessary to discriminate between

home trade and foreign trade. We propose to examine the effect on foreign trade later on when dealing with exchange and import restrictions. As to its effect upon home trade, we have already pointed out that the lack of adequate credit expansion and the possibility of higher interest rates would tend to cause a contraction rather than an increase.

The "stabilisation party" builds its hopes largely upon the psychological effects of stabilisation. In doing so they feel themselves on safe ground, since confidence is the most incalculable of all factors and it is impossible to foresee for certain how the public will react to stabilisation. Anyone with unbiassed views and a little expert knowledge must realise that stabilisation in circumstances which perpetuate disequilibrium, both internally through excessive indebtedness and internationally through a discrepancy between price-levels, cannot last. It is nevertheless just possible that the public might be misled by the appearance of stability on the surface. It was thoroughly misled during the period between 1925 and 1929, and even though the events of the last six years should have taught the world a lesson, the memory of many people is short. It is, therefore, just conceivable that stabilisation might be followed by a boom similar to that of 1929. As, however, the fundamental causes of disequilibrium which were responsible for the collapse of 1929–1931 would be, for the most part, still in existence, the boom would inevitably end in a fresh crisis. It is infinitely more probable, however, that no boom would take place. On the contrary, home trade, at any rate in Great Britain and in countries which at present enjoy a reasonable degree of prosperity, would contract. Nor would the home trade of countries with gold currencies improve after stabilisation unless it were accompanied by a devaluation of those currencies.

## (6) EFFECT ON HOME TRADE

Even those among the adherents of immediate stabilisation who are realistic enough to admit that if sterling were to be stabilised there would be a contraction in home trade, argue that this country in particular, and the world in general, would be amply compensated by the expansion in foreign trade. Some of them admit that possibly the expansion in foreign trade would not be quite as large as the contraction in home trade, but in their opinion true prosperity can only be based on increased international interchange of goods and to that end it would be worth while to sacrifice part of the internal turnover. Those who think this way prefer a bird in the bush to several birds in the hand. For it is far from certain that international stabilisation would be accompanied by the revival of foreign trade they anticipate. The adverse effect of fluctuating exchanges on international trade is grossly exaggerated. Merchants engaged in foreign trade are in a position to cover their exchange risks, and the extent to which this necessity discourages foreign trade cannot be very large. Consequently the revival of foreign trade that directly resulted from exchange stability would be relatively modest.

Adherents of immediate stabilisation argue, however, that in addition to the direct effect of exchange stability, international stabilisation would lead to an expansion of international trade through the elimination of various exchange and import restrictions. Whether this would be so would depend largely upon the circumstances in which stabilisation took place. If it were to leave some currencies overvalued, the countries concerned would have to continue to defend themselves with the aid of tariffs, quotas, and exchange restrictions. Countries whose currencies were not overvalued would not be under the same necessity, but as a retaliation or as bargaining counters, they would also probably be forced to retain import restrictions. Financially weak countries, whether or not their currencies were overvalued, would equally be inclined to be on the safe side and to retain their exchange restrictions for years after the exchanges had been stabilised—as indeed they did during the period of post-war stabilisation.

In any case, to a large extent Government intervention in foreign commercial and financial transactions has come to stay. As a result of the crisis most countries have become less dependent upon the caprices of international trade and world conditions than they were before 1929. Few Governments are likely to assume responsibility for restoring the previous state of affairs. And few countries are likely to return to the *laissez-faire* doctrine, according to which a country can and should import recklessly and trust to luck that its exports will take care of themselves. While it is probable that a return to the gold standard would strengthen the forces of orthodoxy and stop or even reverse the trend towards Government intervention, there is not the least likelihood of a return to the old system of *laissez-faire*.

The setback that would be caused by stabilisation to the trend towards the planning of foreign trade and to planning in general is used by the adherents of immediate stabilisation as a powerful argument in support of their policy. In the author's view, however, this is one of the main arguments against premature stabilisation. Notwithstanding all its disastrous effects, the crisis has served a useful purpose in encouraging the tendency towards the development of a rational economic system. The orthodox camp may object that it is not worth while to obtain prosperity at the cost of liberty. In reality, the choice is not between sacrificing liberty or retaining it, but between consenting to certain restrictions to freedom through planning or having to put up with them as a result of the collapse of the capitalist system. Those who are not particularly impressed by the necessity of improving the standard of living of the poor classes may conceivably pay more heed to this argument. It is, however, entirely a matter of opinion whether the instability of the exchanges should be debited or credited on that account.

### (7) THE INFLATION BOGY

The relatively moderate wing of the orthodox camp, while admitting that stabilisation would entail higher interest rates, regards this as a necessary evil and maintains that it would be worth putting up with. The extreme orthodox wing, on the other hand, holds the view that higher interest rates would be a blessing for their own sake and that it would be wise to stabilise in order to put an end to the period of cheap money. Here we are confronted with fanatics who consider every slight improvement in trade unsound, and who never feel safe and happy unless the world is down at the deepest point of depression. The moment there is a slight recovery from that point, they utter frantic warnings that we are in the middle of a dangerous inflation. To their minds, it would be desirable to check any tendency towards expansion, and the restoration of the gold standard in the existing circumstances would provide an excellent opportunity for such a policy.

To add weight to this argument, the adherents of immediate stabilisation usually exaggerate beyond measure the dangers of uncontrolled inflation in the existing state of affairs. They are aware that to argue against a trade revival by means of cheap money after six years of severe depression is like discussing the dangers of icebergs with inhabitants of the Sahara. On the other hand, the horrors of post-war inflation are still fresh in the minds of this generation and can be used for stabilisationist propaganda. They argue that if a currency remains inconvertible, sooner or later the Government, Parliament, and public are bound to yield to the temptation to inflate on a large scale, and that as a result the pound will share the fate of the German mark. The fact that the budgetary policy of the British Government has been more orthodox than that of any Government on the gold standard does not prevent them from using such arguments. They trust that their readers or audiences will not realise the immense difference between present circumstances and those in which inflation took place in Central Europe after the war. Without enlarging upon this aspect of the subject, let it be sufficient to point out that, even if the British Government were to decide upon inflationary expenditure, in existing circumstances the pound would not be affected by it any more than the dollar has been affected by President Roosevelt's gigantic inflationary expenditure.

C

In any case, the question does not arise, since the present Government has declared itself against inflation, and a Socialist Government which might be tempted to adopt a different policy would be quite prepared to suspend the gold standard if it had been restored before they came into office.

The armoury of stabilisationists is inexhaustible. If they find that they are appealing in vain to the internationalism of their public, they are prepared to change their attitude at a moment's notice and attempt to appeal to their nationalism. It is argued that, in the case of stabilisation at existing exchange rates, sterling would be at an advantage against a number of currencies and British foreign trade would, therefore, continue to benefit by it. On this ground they urge stabilisation and warn the public that if we wait much longer the Gold Bloc may be forced to devalue and we may then lose the advantage of an undervalued exchange. This is, however, an extremely narrow and short-sighted point of view. So long as equilibrium is not restored, there can be no real stability and prosperity. It would be an amazing lack of statesmanship to sacrifice our chances of a lasting solution for the sake of certain temporary advantages that might be secured by the undervaluation of sterling.

### (8) WHY STABILISATION WOULD BE PREMATURE

Let us now summarise the reasons why stabilisation of sterling at the present stage would be premature.

1. On the basis of existing exchange rates, stabilisation would perpetuate the state of disequilibrium between the price-levels of various countries. Unless and until exchange rates and price-levels

achieve a relative degree of equilibrium by international agreement or otherwise, it would be
unwise to stabilise.

2. The British authorities have to accumulate a gold
   reserve well in excess of their present holding.

3. The policy of cheap money will have to make
   further progress and the bulk of public and
   private indebtedness all over the world will have
   to be converted to a lower basis before the process
   is reversed through stabilisation.

4. There can be no stabilisation unless and until all
   major currencies have been depreciated or devalued well below their present gold values, so
   as to make the burden of indebtedness more
   bearable.

5. It would not be advisable to stabilise unless and
   until the principles of economic planning have
   been safely established so as to avoid the risk of
   a relapse into economic anarchy as a result of the
   return to gold.

6. It would be unsafe to stabilise until conditions for
   international co-operation have become more
   favourable, or alternatively, until conditions are
   such as to make stability independent of international co-operation.

7. It would not be advisable to stabilise until the
   public of this and other countries have adequate
   guarantees that the gold standard will hence-
   forward be managed in a truly unorthodox spirit.

The necessity of establishing equilibrium between
exchanges and price-levels before stabilising is too
obvious to require any addition to what we have
already remarked on the subject earlier in this article.
It would be an unpardonable mistake to take the

plunge of stabilising and to trust to luck that everything would straighten out in the course of time.

The necessity of a large British gold reserve in the
interest not only of the stability of sterling, but of
international currencies generally, should be obvious
to every student of recent monetary history. Unless
sterling is technically strong and above suspicion,
London cannot satisfactorily fulfil her task as the
world's banking centre, and the international financial
structure will remain exposed to violent shocks.

### (9) POLICY OF CHEAP MONEY

Although the policy of cheap money has made progress during the last three years, it is still far from
having achieved everything it should. It is confined to
a small number of countries, and even within those
countries mainly to Government securities. In Great
Britain, for instance, mortgages, industrial debentures,
etc., have not sufficiently benefited by the policy of
cheap money. Only if and when Government loans are
on a $2\frac{1}{2}$ per cent basis and other interest rates have
adjusted themselves to this level can this country
afford to expose itself to a reversal in the trend of
money rates.

While such a reduction in interest rates would reduce
considerably the real burden of the interest on public
and private indebtedness, it would leave the capital
burden unchanged. Before we could afford to stabilise,
it would be advisable to achieve a material reduction
in this capital burden, or, at any rate, to secure conditions in which it would be reasonable to assume that
such a reduction would take place after stabilisation.
The only safe way to achieve that end would be to

depreciate and subsequently devalue all currencies well below their present levels. In doing so we should open the way to a material increase in commodity prices, or alternatively, to a material increase in production. In either case, the absolute burden of the indebtedness, or its relative burden by comparison with the volume of real wealth, would be reduced.

The economic crisis has made the world realise the necessity for a much higher degree of Government intervention than had previously existed in most countries. This intervention is considered by most people as a temporary tendency and the moment monetary stability is restored there will be a sweeping demand for its elimination. As a result, the progress towards a more rational system would be reversed and the good results achieved from the wreck of the crisis destroyed. The longer the present period is prolonged, the more the public will become used to the measures of intervention. Moreover, these measures will tend to improve by trial and error and will end by becoming less unpopular. If stabilisation is postponed for a sufficient number of years, the progress towards planning will have got sufficiently on its way to resist the reactionary tendency stabilisation would provoke. It would be well worth postponing stabilisation for the sake of securing the establishment of a system that would be better equipped to safeguard the world from shocks than the system which prevailed before the crisis.

## (10) NO RETURN TO ORTHODOXY

The present moment is anything but suitable for the establishment of genuine international co-operation in the interest of stabilisation. To mention only one

example, President Roosevelt can hardly afford to
adopt an international attitude before the presidential
election of November 1936. There are other material
obstacles in the way of international co-operation.
Their elimination is essential if we want to stabilise.
If it appears that genuine international co-operation
cannot be hoped for, we can only hope to achieve
stabilisation in conditions in which its maintenance
will remain relatively independent of international
co-operation, just as it was before the war. To that end,
it is essential to wait until a more equitable redistribu-
tion of gold takes place, and until an adequate depreciation of all currencies has raised the value of various
gold reserves to a sufficiently high level.

Lastly, it is essential that the world should be safe-
guarded against a return to monetary orthodoxy with
the restoration of monetary stability. The restoration
of stability ought not to be an obstacle to planned
economic expansion. It would not be safe to stabilise
until the management of the monetary policy of various
countries is in the hands of people sufficiently adaptable to realise the change in the world trend and who
would not be enslaved to orthodox doctrines. Only then
should there be a restoration of international monetary
stability. Even so stability should not mean rigidity.
Currencies should be allowed a wider scope for fluctuations than before the crisis. Stabilisation should also
be based on the understanding that should existing
parities prove inconvenient, they could be adjusted to
meet requirements.

Admittedly, it may take several years before the
conditions required for stabilisation are fulfilled. It
would be better, however, to put up with the inconvenience of comparative monetary instability rather

than to expose ourselves to the dangers of premature stabilisation. The world can ill afford to allow a second collapse similar to that of 1931 to take place within the lifetime of the present generation. Such a collapse might easily lead to the conclusion that something was fundamentally wrong with the whole economic and social system, and the discontent thus arising might lead to the collapse of our civilisation. To be safe-guarded against such a disaster, it would be well worth our while to wait a little longer before returning to monetary stability.

# THE FINANCIAL TRIANGLE

## (1) STERLING—DOLLAR—FRANC

THE subject of the present essay is the eternal triangle
which seems to have been inherited from the novelists
by writers on financial subjects. Ever since 1933, anyone attempting to devise a solution to the international
monetary problem has found himself confronted with
the sterling-dollar-franc triangle. These three major
currencies appear to be hopelessly out of equilibrium
with each other. Unless a certain degree of equilibrium
is established between them there is little hope of
coming to an international understanding for stabilisation, and still less hope of making any understanding
that might possibly be concluded work successfully.

It is evident that, as things are at present, the franc
is hopelessly overvalued and the dollar hopelessly
undervalued in relation to sterling. A return to the
gold standard in such circumstances would perpetuate
the adverse pressure on the franc and on the currencies
of the Gold Bloc in general. It would equally perpetuate the magnetic power of the United States to
draw gold from Europe. Between the two extremes the
position of Great Britain would be one of uncertainty.
With the gold standard restored, London would resume
its rôle as the world's banking centre and the violent
movements caused by the disequilibrium between the
United States and the European continent would inevitably unsettle sterling, especially as its technical
position would remain weaker than either that of the

dollar or of the franc. From time to time, sterling would be exposed to selling pressure, which would necessitate the penalising of British industries by a high bank rate and a contraction of credit. This is why the Chancellor of the Exchequer has repeatedly declared that under the existing circumstances he is not prepared to stabilise sterling.

## (2) NEW BRITISH POLICY

To be able to see the international monetary deadlock in its true light, it is important to understand that in official British quarters the overvaluation of the franc in relation to sterling is considered just as grave an obstacle to stabilisation as the undervaluation of the dollar. This is the point which continental opinion has failed so far to appreciate. They understood readily enough when Great Britain aimed at obtaining the highest possible degree of undervaluation of sterling in relation to the largest possible number of currencies. Human nature being what it is, continental opinion regarded it as natural that British statesmen should desire to obtain for British exporters the greatest possible advantages in the form of an undervalued currency. British opinion went through that phase of primitive greed which was a natural reaction from the disadvantages Great Britain had had to put up with before September 1931 owing to the overvaluation of sterling. Having lost export markets and exhausted the gold reserve in the defence of sterling at an overvalued parity, it is easily understandable that Great Britain should have aimed at preventing a recurrence of these disadvantages by obtaining the highest possible degree of undervaluation for sterling. It is more difficult to understand the change that has taken place in the official British attitude since the end of last year. It is no longer a gross undervaluation of sterling that is aimed at. To that end, it would be a comparatively simple matter to depreciate sterling in relation to the dollar by another 5 to 10 per cent. Assuming that the United States should not retaliate by a fresh devaluation of the dollar, such a move would put sterling in an enviable position, since it would become undervalued in terms of every currency apart from the yen and the currencies of the Sterling Bloc. A year ago such a solution would presumably have appeared satisfactory in official British quarters. To-day, however, it would be regarded as only a half-solution. The other half of the problem, the gross overvaluation of the franc, would remain unsolved.

It may be argued that from a purely British point of view it matters little if France chooses to penalise herself by an overvalued currency. So long as sterling is undervalued in terms of practically all important currencies there is no need for Great Britain to fear any inconvenience. The experience of the period between 1925 and 1931 has, however, taught Great Britain that the existence of one single important currency which is overvalued is sufficient to create a dangerous position in the sphere of international finance. In 1931 it was the weak position of the pound that brought upon the world the international financial crisis which ended by affecting the countries with strong currencies. In a few years' time an overvalued franc would lead to another international financial crisis which would react upon sterling even though its own position were strong and sound. Moreover,

Great Britain has no desire to put up with any deflation, and for this reason she is not prepared to stabilise in circumstances in which an important group of countries would have to continue to deflate in order to try to restore equilibrium. The effects of such deflationary pressure would not be confined within the borders of the countries which were directly concerned. The movement for deflation might easily assume world-wide character and this is what Great Britain is anxious to avoid. So long as sterling is not tied to gold, the effect of deflation abroad can always be countered by allowing sterling to depreciate further. Once, however, the pound is linked to gold, Great Britain will be under the influence of the deflationary monetary policy pursued by other countries.

## (3) HOW TO ATTAIN EQUILIBRIUM

This explains why Great Britain wishes to avoid stabilising prematurely, that is, stabilising unless and until world conditions are such as to make it reasonably certain that stabilisation will not be followed either by world-wide deflation or by pressure on sterling. As things are, Great Britain has no reason to be dissatisfied with the state of her trade. It is true that the number of unemployed is still just under two million. At the same time the index of industrial production is now well up to its 1929 level and agricultural production has also increased since the beginning of the crisis. This means that although the number of workmen engaged in production is smaller than it was at the time of the boom, their output is if anything larger, and this leads to the conclusion that the higher figure of unemployment is due, not to the depressed state of trade, but to the increased efficiency of production and to the larger number of those employable. In the circumstances, stabilisation for Great Britain would mean risking this relatively high degree of prosperity. It would be a leap in the dark which the Government is not prepared to undertake unless and until equilibrium between British, French, and American prices has been restored. This equilibrium can be restored in four different ways:

1. By allowing sterling to depreciate in relation to the dollar to the extent of some 5 to 10 per cent, and devaluing the franc to an extent corresponding to its economic parity with sterling at this lower level.

2. By raising the exchange value of both sterling and the dollar to their economic parities in relation to the franc, which would mean a more pronounced appreciation for the dollar than for sterling.

3. By a rise in commodity prices in Great Britain and to a larger extent in the United States.

4. By a slight fall of commodity prices in Great Britain and a substantial fall of commodity prices in France.

The first solution is the one favoured by British opinion. It is, however, opposed by official quarters both in France and in the United States. In France, until recently, the idea of an alignment of the franc to sterling and the dollar was viewed favourably in highly influential quarters even though it was never openly supported in official quarters. The recent success of the French authorities in checking the run on the franc, however, changed the French attitude in this respect to no slight extent. It is now maintained that the adjustment of the currencies should take place not through a devaluation of the franc but through an increase in the exchange value of both sterling and the dollar. This solution does not meet with unanimous approval even in France, where a large section of competent opinion favours a downward adjustment of the franc in connection with a general stabilisation scheme for all currencies. It is entirely inacceptable from a British and American point of view, since it would involve a high degree of deflation, which the two countries are certainly not prepared to put up with. Even the extremists of monetary orthodoxy in Great Britain do not go further than to demand the immediate stabilisation of sterling at its present value. Nobody thinks of suggesting that stabilisation should be preceded by an appreciation of sterling in relation to gold. As for the United States, it is simply unthinkable that President Roosevelt would be prepared to engineer deflation for international considerations on the eve of a presidential election. Thus, the second solution may be ruled out as impracticable.

## (4) THE AMERICAN ATTITUDE

The attitude of the United States towards the problem of the adjustment of currencies to their economic parities constitutes a very important obstacle to any early stabilisation. It is inspired by the same selfishness that characterised the British attitude during the early years of the crisis. As we pointed out above, immediately after the suspension of the gold standard, Great Britain aimed at securing for herself the highest possible degree of commercial advantage by a maximum undervaluation of sterling. Subsequently this attitude has changed, and now the British aim is to restore equilibrium between the major currencies. The American aim, however, is still to secure the most advantageous position for the United States by an undervaluation of the dollar. In the case of Great Britain the desire to stabilise sterling at a level at which the trade balance might tend to improve was understandable, since the technical position of sterling was none too strong and the trade balance was unfavourable. In the case of the United States, however, the necessity to defend the dollar by stabilising at an undervalued level does not arise. The United States has a huge gold reserve and her trade balance is extremely favourable. In the course of 1934 the United States was able to import one milliard dollars of gold, which shows the extent to which the existing level of the dollar is in her favour. In his recent broadcast address, Mr Morgenthau, Secretary to the United States Treasury, stated that the United States wants to stabilise in conditions which will enable her to retain her "fair share" of the world's trade and of the world's stock of gold. If an annual surplus of one milliard dollars is considered in Washington to be a fair share, there is indeed no common basis for negotiations with the United States. Europe would be unable to stand the strain of such a surplus at her expense, and sooner or later there would be another financial collapse. The only way to avoid this would be to stabilise at a level which is less in favour of the United States and which would, therefore, tend to reduce the American export surplus. The Washington Administration is, however, not prepared to agree to such stabilisation. As Mr Morgenthau stated, he is prepared to stabilise provided that none of the other currencies is depreciated any further. This attitude rules out the possibility of the first solution being brought about by agreement. Unless the United States and France change their attitude, the first solution will be as impracticable as the second.

Towards the end of 1934, financial experts within and outside the Gold Bloc attached sanguine hopes to the possibility of arriving at the third solution, namely, that of a rise in world prices which would restore equilibrium between sterling, dollar, and franc. Indeed, one of the main arguments both against devaluation and deflation within the Gold Bloc was that there was no need to take any such drastic steps, since a rise in world prices, which was considered imminent, would in any case cancel out the overvaluation of the gold currencies. Six months have passed since these prophecies were made and there has been so far no sign of any such rise in prices. It is true that President Roosevelt is undertaking ambitious public works, and these together with his silver policy are calculated, in theory at any rate, to raise prices. Practical experience in the past in this respect is, however, anything but encouraging. The best that can reasonably be hoped is that through his inflationary measures President Roosevelt will be able to prevent the fall in American prices that would otherwise take place.

### (5) DEFLATION IN FRANCE

The outlook regarding world prices is thus such as to make it reasonable to rule out the third solution as being unlikely. There remains the fourth solution, which is deflationary efforts on the part of the Gold Bloc, and to a much less extent on the part of Great Britain, in order to restore equilibrium. As far as Great

Britain is concerned, no deflationary efforts are likely to be undertaken. In some of the countries of the Gold Bloc, on the other hand, preparations have been made for another desperate deflationary drive. In France in particular, M. Flandin's anti-deflationary policy having been defeated by the Bank of France, the new Government has resumed deflation. The Government is making an attempt to restrict purchasing power by means of budgetary economies and certain prices have been cut by decree. The question is whether these efforts can go sufficiently far to bring about a fall in French commodity prices to the extent of some 25 per cent, which is the minimum required to restore the equilibrium between French prices and the world level. The answer is most emphatically in the negative. Deflation in France is already in such an advanced state that any further efforts in that direction will defeat their own object. The desperate state of the Treasury will in itself prevent orthodox deflation from proceeding much further. The curtailment of purchasing power as a consequence of economies and cuts in prices are bound to react unfavourably upon trade and are bound to reduce taxation revenue. It will be utterly impossible to balance the budget. It will not be easy for the Treasury to cover the deficit by means of borrowing. The experience of the crisis of May has proved that a difficult Treasury position can automatically prevent the Bank of France from enforcing a policy of credit restriction. Owing to the withdrawals of deposits from the banks, the latter were not prepared to renew their Treasury bills and the Bank of France had to come to the rescue of the Treasury by providing the banks with the means required so as to induce them to carry the Treasury bills they held. It is evident that the stage at which deflation in France will reduce itself *ad absurdum* is not far off. There is not the least hope that they will be able to enforce a sufficient fall in commodity prices to restore the desired equilibrium.

What then will be the outcome of the present deadlock? If none of the four solutions is practicable, how will the sterling-dollar-franc triangle be brought into equilibrium? According to some people, what is wanted is to resume the economic conference which broke down in 1933, in the hope that this time some understanding may be reached. As things are, however, there is absolutely no common basis to the British, French, and American points of view. To resume the economic conference in present conditions would be to invite failure, and a second failure in this sphere would discourage attempts at an understanding at a future time when conditions might be more hopeful than at present. The world will overcome the deadlock, not by resorting to an international conference, but by the natural trend of developments. Sooner or later, France will realise that it is futile to attempt to bolster up her currency at its present level. Possibly in her stubbornness she may wait until as a result of a succession of crises the technical position of the franc has been weakened to such an extent as to make further resistance impossible. Possibly she will adopt a more reasonable attitude and will take the opportunity of the next crisis to work out her own salvation by following the example of Belgium. Once the franc has been devalued, the problem of solving the currency deadlock will have been considerably simplified. But there will still remain the British-American controversy over the sterling-dollar rate of stabilisation. In the course of time, however, there is reason to hope that the American attitude will become

D

more reasonable, and that the Washington Administration will no longer insist upon a solution which would impose an intolerable drain upon Europe's gold resources. While at present Mr Morgenthau threatens reprisals if any other currency depreciates, once he is confronted with a *fait accompli* he will probably accept it.

One thing is certain. It is not to the interest of either France or the United States to induce Great Britain to stabilise in circumstances which would leave the pound vulnerable. This was done once in 1925 and the whole world had to pay for the mistake. To avoid the repetition of this mistake would be to the interest not only of Great Britain but also of the rest of the world. London cannot adequately fulfil her function as the world's banking centre unless the pound is safe and above suspicion. Nor would there be any hope of maintaining a newly restored sterling parity unless each of the three angles of the sterling-dollar-franc triangle could be safely relied upon.

# MR MONTAGU NORMAN'S POLICY

## (1) CHANGES SINCE 1932

IN October 1932 the author published a book entitled *Montagu Norman : A Study in Financial Statesmanship*. It was an attempt to explain the policy of one of the most discussed and least understood personalities of our generation. While essentially critical in detail, the author endeavoured to regard the Governor's policy with sympathy and understanding. He attempted to describe how Mr Norman during ten fateful years endeavoured to steer between the Scylla of extreme orthodoxy and the Charybdis of radicalism. The author presented Mr Norman's attitude towards Central European reconstruction, and his conflict with France as the result of this attitude, as a manifestation of the traditional British balance-of-power policy of which he regarded Mr Norman as a true representative.

Nearly three years have passed since the author put the finishing touches to his interpretation of Mr Montagu Norman. Those three eventful years have provided a severe test for anyone in a responsible position. The author has decided to re-examine, in the light of this experience, his views on Mr Norman's policy. The task is by no means easy, for in the author's mind there is no common basis of comparison between Mr Norman of 1932 and Mr Norman of 1935. In the course of three years, the author himself has changed considerably his attitude towards monetary policy. While he has never been an adherent of the strictly orthodox school, under the influence of developments in recent years he has departed considerably from the classical doctrines of the nineteenth century. While until 1932 he was on the whole in agreement with the broad principles of Mr Norman's policy, to-day he is definitely on the other side of the barricade.

Notwithstanding his change of opinion, the author feels he can state without hesitation that he has the same admiration for the Governor as he had three years ago. One cannot help but admire such an outstanding example of a remarkable type. The fact that the author has arrived at the conclusion that, in the changed conditions, Mr Norman has become an anachronism does not in any way diminish his sincere admiration for that strong and silent man. It is true that during the last three years Mr Norman has departed more than once from his proverbial silence. On almost every occasion when he spoke in public, according to the unanimous opinion of his friends and enemies, he confirmed the rule that silence is golden and he made many of us regret that he had chosen to suspend this golden standard. While the Governor has done a good deal to destroy his prestige as a silent man, he certainly has made up for the loss by increasing his reputation as a strong man. He has also enhanced his reputation as the upholder of orthodox tradition in British monetary policy in the most difficult circumstances. Whether or not we agree with his policy, we cannot help admiring him for it.

The developments that followed the suspension of the gold standard in 1931 placed the Bank of England at a disadvantage against the Treasury. The fact that most of the merchant banking firms which control the Bank had become hopelessly immobilised through the German crisis, prevented them from insisting too strongly upon the independence of the Bank. Legally, the status of the Bank of England has not changed. It is still a private corporation which is technically in a position to raise the bank rate and restrict credit should the majority of its Directors decide to do so. In reality, however, these Directors are well aware that in the case of a repudiation of Standstill credits by Germany, the existence of most of the firms they represent would depend on the goodwill of the Treasury. The Bank of England itself had to fall back upon the Treasury for the "mobilisation" of the £5,000,000 it had lent to Austria in 1931. In the circumstances, the Central Bank has been hardly in a position to insist upon its right to determine the monetary policy of the country.

Moreover, with the establishment of the Exchange Equalisation Account, the Treasury has created for its use an instrument by which it was well in a position to neutralise any unwanted move on the part of the Bank of England. It is true that the Exchange Equalisation Account has been operated through the Bank of England, but the latter has acted merely as an agent for the Treasury and has had to carry out instructions received from Whitehall.

## (2) MR NORMAN'S INFLUENCE

In the circumstances, it is surprising that Mr Norman has succeeded in retaining at least part of his power. It is an open secret that ever since the crisis there has been a tug-of-war between the Treasury and the Bank of England. The Treasury has adopted all

along a much more unorthodox view than the Bank.
If Mr Norman had had his way we should have re-
stabilised sterling sometime in the autumn of 1931, and
at a rate at which it would have been, if anything,
somewhat overvalued. The Treasury was, however,
anxious to avoid a repetition of the mistake of 1925.
Since the question of stabilisation is an act of Government, Mr Norman was powerless to impose his view
on the Treasury. On the other hand, it is widely
believed that his influence on the details of the execution of the Government's monetary policy has been
considerable. Whenever a depreciating trend of sterling
is resisted at the cost of depleting the gold resources
of the Exchange Equalisation Account, Mr Norman's
influence is suspected behind the policy. Whenever sterling is allowed to appreciate and the Exchange Equalisation Account fails to take advantage of the strong
demand for sterling to acquire the largest possible
amount of gold, Mr Norman's influence is again suspected.

He has been, however, none too successful until
recently in his attitude towards the Government's
policy of cheap money. Ever since 1932 he is known
to have viewed that policy with strong disapproval.
He did not believe in the success of the great conversion operation which, it is said, was undertaken against
his advice. In all fairness it must be pointed out that,
once the policy was decided upon, Mr Norman col-
laborated loyally in its execution. In this respect, his
attitude has compared favourably with that taken
by the Bank of France towards M. Flandin's policy
of cheap money, which was frustrated by the passive
resistance of the regents and high officials of the
French Central Bank. While Mr Norman may put up

a fight against a policy he disapproves of, he certainly cannot be accused of attempting to sabotage it. At the same time, his unwillingness to swim with the tide has made collaboration with Whitehall more difficult. Loyalty in itself does not always make good an evident lack of enthusiasm for the official policy. Mr Norman's stubborn refusal to forget something of what were regarded as dogmas in 1931 and to learn something new instead has exasperated Treasury officials and Cabinet Ministers alike. On one occasion, a Conservative member of the Cabinet is known to have exclaimed: "Norman has finished for ever the chances of independent Central Banking".

### (3) END OF INDEPENDENT CENTRAL BANKING

This leads us to one of the principal shortcomings of the Governor which was repeatedly pointed out in *Montagu Norman: A Study in Financial Statesmanship.* Mr Norman is not a good diplomatist. Although in many ways he is very subtle, he has the failing of not knowing when he is defeated. He is an enthusiastic believer in independent Central Banking, and yet through his attitude he has been doing his utmost to reduce the chances that the independence of the Bank of England may ever be restored to what it was before the crisis. Admittedly, in any case, he is fighting a losing battle. Independent Central Banking in our days is a glaring anachronism. It was only possible at a time when Government interference was negligible in every sphere of the economic system and when the monetary system worked so smoothly as to require little more than formal supervision.

Mr Norman appears to have failed to realise the

trend of evolution affecting Central Banking. He has not realised that Central Banking is no longer the private concern of a small group of merchant bankers or even of a somewhat larger group of stockholders. It has become one of the most essential functions of the modern State, and as such it cannot escape Parliamentary control. Before the crisis, whenever in the House of Commons a question was asked concerning the Bank of England, the Chancellor of the Exchequer or his spokesman answered that the Bank was a private corporation and the Government was not responsible for its business. Any such answer at the present time would arouse indignation even among the majority supporting the Government. The principle that the monetary policy of the country is the private affair of the directors or stockholders of a bank has become inadmissible.

It is of course only natural that Mr Norman, who has devoted his life to independent Central Banking, should be most unwilling to bow his head to the change. With the aid of his unquestionable prestige he would doubtless be able to postpone the change in the status of the Bank if only he would play his hand well. The British nation is not in favour of violent changes, and is fond of upholding the traditions of institutions at any rate in external form if not in substance. If Mr Norman would only try to swim with the tide instead of against it, there is no reason to suppose that there would be a change in the status of the Bank for many years to come. If, on the other hand, he should insist on rubbing Government, Parliament, and public opinion the wrong way, the inevitable result will be the nationalisation of the Bank.

The growing unpopularity of the Bank of England

outside the City is largely the result of Mr Norman's well-known policy in favour of a premature stabilisation of sterling. He is supposed to be using all his influence to that end. This may appear to be in the interests of the international banking community of London, but is certainly not in the interests of the country as a whole. To do justice to him, it is necessary to emphasise that he is convinced that in serving the interests of the banking community he serves at the same time the interests of the whole country. He is far too public-spirited to desire to sacrifice the interests of the whole community for the sake of a fraction of it. Nor are the bankers whose interests his policy serves in any way more selfish than any other class. Indeed, they are as fine a set of men as one can find anywhere. Their tragedy and that of Mr Norman is that they have forgotten nothing and have learnt nothing since 1931. They still possess the same international mentality which may have been fully justified before the crisis, but has become entirely unjustified in the light of the experience of the last few years.

## (4) "INTERNATIONALISM" OF THE CITY

In one of his public speeches Mr Norman remarked that, although admittedly home trade had improved, "we in the City are largely international" and cannot regain our prosperity without a recovery in international trade. He does not realise that the prosperity of the country no longer depends upon international trade to anything like the extent that it did a few years ago. Notwithstanding the fact that the index of industrial production in the first quarter of 1935 was 5 per cent above the boom year of 1929, he still seems

to believe that, in the absence of a substantial revival
in foreign trade, this country is bound to suffer perpetual depression. It is this misconception that has
been responsible for his mistaken monetary policy.
He is struggling for stabilisation in the hope that the
result will be a revival in foreign trade. Although
he may be vaguely aware that such a revival could only
be achieved at the cost of a decline in home trade, he
seems to consider it worth while to sacrifice a certain
amount of home trade for the sake of an increase in
the foreign trade. In any case, according to his conception, it is contrary to the laws of nature that home
trade should be prosperous while foreign trade should
remain depressed. If the volume of home trade is to-day
considerably higher than in 1929 while that of foreign
trade is a mere fraction of its pre-crisis figure, then,
in the opinion of those who think like Mr Norman,
something must be wrong with home trade. The increased home trade activity is viewed at the Bank
of England with growing concern and is considered
essentially unsound. In fact, it is alleged that in
February this year Mr Norman, alarmed by the rapid
expansion of home trade, wanted to raise the bank
rate, but was prevented from doing so by the Treasury.

Mr Norman, like so many others of the orthodox
school, does not realise that the change in the proportion between home and foreign trade which began as
a temporary and abnormal movement has become the
new permanent basis of the world's economic system.
Every country has made arrangements to settle down
on this new basis by reducing the extent to which it
is dependent for its prosperity on international trade.
Whether this tendency is good or evil is a matter for
discussion, but that it has gone a long way is an

accomplished fact which ought to be taken into account by those responsible for economic and monetary policy. It would be futile to aim at restoring the old proportion of foreign to home trade in the changed world situation.

### (5) MR NORMAN AND STABILISATION

And yet this is exactly what Mr Norman's policy seems to be aiming at. He is in favour of immediate stabilisation, presumably because he thinks that as a result the pre-crisis proportion between home trade and foreign trade could be restored, partly through a reduction of the former and partly through an increase in the latter. Apparently he has failed to realise that, from the point of view of the country as a whole, the advantages of a moderate increase in foreign trade through stabilisation would be more than outweighed by the cost of stabilisation in the form of loss of home trade through higher interest rates and credit restriction.

Even from the point of view of the City, it is shortsighted to urge stabilisation in circumstances which do not warrant the assumption that stability could be maintained for any length of time. Those who like Mr Norman believe in the gold standard should do their utmost to avoid a second breakdown which might be fatal to the system. Instead of urging the Government to stabilise, they ought to use their influence to prevent the Government from stabilising except in circumstances which provide maximum guarantees for the relatively smooth working of the system. In practice, Mr Norman and those who want to stabilise immediately are much greater dangers to the gold standard than the opponents of the system. The latter in agitating against stabilisation tend to postpone that step until such time as it can be undertaken with the minimum amount of risk. The orthodox school, on the other hand, insist upon a return to gold in circumstances which would inevitably result in discrediting the system before many years were past.

Mr Norman's attitude towards stabilisation would be understandable if he belonged to the extreme orthodox school. In reality, before the crisis he showed much willingness to make allowances for practical requirements. In defiance of the fundamental principle of the gold standard, he did not attempt to bring about an adjustment of British prices and costs to the world level by means of an abnormally high bank rate and drastic credit restriction. He was aware that such a policy would be suicidal, since the country simply would not have it. Is there any reason to assume that public opinion in this country is now more willing to put up with deflationary methods than it was before 1931? On the contrary, the experience of the last few years has opened the eyes of large sections of the public who before the crisis were not in a position to see the connection between monetary policy and economic prosperity. It is more essential than ever that when this country returns to the gold standard it should do so in circumstances that will obviate the necessity of having to defend the stability of sterling by an abnormally high bank rate and credit restrictions.


## (6) MR NORMAN'S FOREIGN POLICY

With regard to Mr Norman's foreign policy, the author must admit that his original interpretation has proved to be entirely wrong. The theory that Mr Norman's attitude towards Germany and France was guided consciously or otherwise by the traditional British balance-of-power policy has become untenable in the light of the experience of the last two years. Reviewing *Montagu Norman: A Study in Financial Statesmanship* in the columns of the *New Statesman*, Dr. Hugh Dalton suggested that Mr Norman was simply anti-French and nothing more. This interpretation, though nearer the truth than the author's balance-of-power theory, has also proved to be incorrect. The right interpretation is that Mr Norman is not so much anti-French as pro-German. The fact that he went out of his way to assist France in June 1935 by discouraging speculation against the franc shows that his desire to support the Gold Bloc was stronger than any anti-French feeling he may possibly have harboured. His pro-German sentiments became amply evident during the second half of 1934 when, notwithstanding the partial default on Germany's external debt, he remained anxious to assist Germany. The Bank of England, in fact, granted the Reichsbank a credit of £750,000, which, though nominally was to serve the purpose of unfreezing British commercial claims, led in practice to the extension of new commercial credits to Germany and provided a welcome relief to Dr. Schacht at a time when he was hard pressed for exchange to cover raw material imports. While prior to 1931 any such support for Germany could have been explained on the basis of the balance-of-power policy, in 1934 that explanation was obviously untenable, since in the meantime Germany had become decidedly the strongest continental power, and probably the strongest world power. Mr Norman was in favour of supporting

Germany while she was down, but he appears to be equally in favour of supporting her when, far from being down any longer, she has become a danger to the world's peace.

If the author were to rewrite his book on Mr Norman to-day, it would differ in many respects from what he wrote three years ago. It would be much more critical of Mr Norman's policy. Nevertheless, it would remain complimentary to his character. It would attack Mr Norman's attitude but would pay tribute to his good intentions, his strength, and ability. The author cannot help hoping that Mr Norman will sooner or later realise that it is to the interest of his country and his bank alike to make allowances for the changed situation and modify his attitude accordingly. If not, he will do irreparable harm to the systems he stands for—the gold standard and independent Central Banking.

# CENTRAL BANKS AND TREASURIES

## (1) CENTRAL BANKS DURING AND AFTER THE WAR

THE controversy about the relations between Central Banks and Treasuries is of relatively recent origin. Before the war the question whether Central Banks should be independent or whether they should be under Government control stirred up but little interest. Whether the Central Bank was a State Bank or a limited company owned by its stockholders, whether its executive officials were elected by the proprietors or were appointed by the Government, in every case there was close collaboration between Treasuries and Central Banks. In normal pre-war conditions, there was no particular reason for a Government to interfere with the policy pursued by the Central Bank, and in the absence of evidence to the contrary it is reasonable to assume that as a general rule the latter's activities were to a high degree free from Treasury interference. For this reason, in several countries, and particularly in England, the conception was allowed to develop that the Central Bank is a private enterprise exactly like any other privately owned banking institute. While it was vaguely admitted that the Central Bank was not primarily a profit-earning concern, and that it was responsible to the public for its policy relating to public interests, the exact nature of its responsibilities had not been defined before the war.

The conception that the Central Bank was a private concern received a severe blow during the war. In all

European belligerent countries, with the exception of
Great Britain, the Central Bank had to lend itself as
the executing hand to inflationary financing of war
expenditure. In Great Britain alone the Government
did not insist that the Central Bank should issue notes
without regard to the statutory requirements of an
adequate gold cover. Instead, the Government itself
issued £1 and 10s. Treasury notes. In every other
country, the Central Bank placed its printing-press at
the Treasury's free disposal. If there was any reluctance
on the part of Central Bank Governors to meet the
demand for additional milliards of notes, their objections were easily overruled. Amidst the conditions
prevailing during the war, considerations of monetary
orthodoxy had to be subordinated to the supreme requirements of national defence, and any Central Bank
Governor who attempted to resist would probably have
been dealt with in the same way as if he had been
obstructing the supply of ammunition to the army.

The independence of Central Banks was to all
intents and purposes suspended during the war. Even
in the case of the Bank of England, the maintenance
of its independence was more apparent than real, since
it was tacitly understood that sooner or later the Bank
would have to take over the issue of currency notes.
Indeed, in 1928 the Bank had to withdraw the currency
notes against its own notes and had to accept Government securities for by far the greater part of the note
cover. Thus, in the final result, there was little difference between the effect of the war on the Bank of
England and on Central Banks which did not succeed
in retaining their independence during the war.

It would be difficult to deny that the suspension of
the independence of Central Banks during the war

was a matter of necessity in the interests of national defence. Unfortunately, the Governments of most continental belligerent countries did not relinquish the power they had acquired during the war. They used and abused it during the post-war years when the willingness of Central Bank Governors to oblige them with a few additional milliards of notes whenever requested to do so obviated the unpleasant necessity of having to balance the budget. Hardly any Central Bank displayed any resistance to the policy of the Governments of using them as the most convenient means of raising funds. Indeed, between 1914 and the various dates at which successive countries stabilised their currencies, Central Banks in Europe were to all intents and purposes Government departments. Their independence was confined to the ordinary routine work, while their policy was entirely subordinated to the Treasury.

## (2) INDEPENDENT CENTRAL BANKING

The disastrous consequences of extreme inflation brought forth a strong reaction affecting the relations between Governments and Central Banks. During the period of post-war stabilisation, between 1923 and 1929, there was a strong movement in favour of securing as far as possible the independence of Central Banks in Europe. Under the guidance of a few outstanding personalities in the Central Banking world, such as Mr Montagu Norman in England, Dr Schacht in Germany, and Governor Strong in New York, banks of issue gained in prestige and influence to no slight extent. In the course of a few years, the movement in favour of independent Central Banks made a remark-

E

able progress. Its aim was to secure for Central Banks complete freedom from Government interference in the management of monetary policy. They were to become a State within the State, which was to owe no allegiance either to the Government or to Parliament, and which was to negotiate with the Treasury on an equal footing. This task was easily achieved in England, thanks to the magnetic personality of Mr Montagu Norman. Between 1922 and 1931 Government interference with the Bank of England was something unthinkable. Indeed, it was the Bank of England that interfered with the Government, not only in the sphere of finance but even in the sphere of foreign policy. The fact that the official policy of the British foreign office under Sir Austen Chamberlain was distinctly pro-French did not prevent the Bank of England from pursuing a definitely pro-German policy which from time to time more than cancelled out the practical effects of the official foreign policy. To give an idea of the degree of independence the Bank of England enjoyed during that period, it is sufficient to quote the fact that on February 6, 1929, the bank rate was raised without even consulting the Government, which was naturally anxious to avoid such a move on the eve of the approaching General Election. Indeed, it may be said that until the suspension of the gold standard in 1931, Mr Norman was an absolute despot who brooked no interference on the part of the Government.

His dream was to secure a similar independence for Central Banks in other countries. Whenever a continental country was reconstructed, thanks to the direct assistance given by the Bank of England or under the auspices of the League of Nations with the influence of the Bank of England in the background, the organisation of an independent Central Bank was one of the preliminary conditions of the assistance. State banks had to be converted into limited companies and the shares had to be sold to the public. The statutes of the new or reconstructed Central Banks were drafted in such a way as to create a watertight defence against Government interference. This was done in Austria, Hungary, Germany (where international control was imposed upon the Reichsbank to make it quite safe from Government interference), Bulgaria, Greece, Estonia, etc. In some cases Governments were reluctant to submit to such a curtailment of their power, but since they needed foreign assistance badly, they had to yield.

By 1929 almost all European Central Banks were reorganised on a basis of technical independence. Even in countries such as France, where the currency was stabilised without any foreign support, it was considered advisable to swim with the tide, especially as Government interference with the Bank of France prior to 1926 had had fatal consequences upon the franc. With the exception of Italy and a few other countries where the existence of dictatorships ruled out the possibility of independent Central Banks, the movement may be said to have succeeded all over Europe. At any rate this was the impression at the time.

The success of the movement in favour of independent Central Banking was crowned by the establishment of the Bank for International Settlements in 1930. One of the objects of this bank was to support Central Banks in their resistance against Government interference. The existence of a powerful central organisation for Central Banks was calculated to strengthen their independence.

## (3) BANK OF ENGLAND AND THE CRISIS

The triumph of Central Banks proved to be, however, short-lived. Events were to prove a little over a year after the establishment of the Bank for International Settlements that independent Central Banking was a fiction. It could only exist in relatively normal conditions when there was no particular inducement for Governments to intervene in matters of monetary policy. The moment the real test came in the form of a financial crisis, the carefully constructed edifice of independent Central Banking collapsed like a house of cards. The series of crises that followed each other in 1931 and subsequent years brought about a complete reversal of the movement in favour of securing the independence of Central Banks. It suffered a heavy blow in its country of origin, England. After the German crisis and the suspension of the gold standard on September 21, 1931, the Bank of England had to relinquish its control over monetary policy. It had to subordinate its activities to the Treasury in everything that was essential.

There were several reasons for this change. In the first place, the failure of the policy of restoring sterling to its pre-war parity and maintaining it there dealt a severe blow to the prestige of the Bank of England and to the personal influence of Mr Norman. The technical position of the Bank of England was also extremely weak at the time of the suspension of the gold standard, since the whole of its gold reserve of £130 million was earmarked to secure the Franco-American credits of a similar amount that had been raised in defence of sterling. What was even more important, as a result of the Central European crisis, the position of most of the merchant banks which control the Bank of England threatened to become critical. The London banking community had lent some £60 million to Germany and other Central European countries which became hopelessly frozen in the summer of 1931. In the case of a number of merchant banks, the amount thus involved was several times larger than their own capital and reserves. It was to be feared that circumstances might arise in which many of these banking houses would have to be supported. Evidently the Bank of England itself was not in a position to provide such a large amount. Its own resources were immobilised to some degree in the form of frozen credits to the Central Banks of Austria, Germany, and Hungary, granted either directly or through the intermediary of the Bank for International Settlements. Although there was no need for any actual support, it was feared that should the necessity for it arise, support could only be forthcoming from the Treasury. This being the case, it was difficult for the Bank of England to make any effort to assert its independence against the authority of one on whose goodwill the fate of the community of London merchant bankers depended.

## (4) BANK v. TREASURY

By far the most important reason for the decline of the influence and independence of the Bank of England was the development of a fundamental difference of opinion between Threadneedle Street and Whitehall. The reason why the Bank of England was able to retain its independence until 1931 was that, generally speaking, its views were largely identical with those of the Treasury on almost every question of major importance. The moment the two authorities drifted apart it was inevitable that the Treasury should prove to be the stronger of the two. This was what actually happened after the suspension of the gold standard. While the Bank of England retained to a large extent its original orthodox attitude towards monetary policy, the Treasury began to take much more realistic views of the situation. The Bank of England would have liked to have re-stabilised sterling as soon as possible and at the highest possible level. The Government, on the other hand, realised the extreme unpopularity of the gold standard and the practical necessity for stimulating trade by allowing sterling to depreciate to its natural level.

Since Whitehall must, of necessity, have the last word, Threadneedle Street had to submit much against its own inclination. It had to lend itself as the executing hand to a policy of which it strongly disapproved. The Treasury's position in relation to the Bank of England was further strengthened by the establishment of the Exchange Equalisation Account, with the aid of which it secured a much higher degree of control over sterling than the Bank of England had ever possessed. All the technical weapons at the disposal of the Bank disappeared into insignificance compared with the huge "fighting fund" at the Treasury's disposal. While the Bank of England's gold reserve remained immobilised, the Treasury assumed a very active and very strong position in the foreign exchange market and even in the internal money market, thanks to the operations of the Exchange Equalisation Account.

Although it was the Bank of England that operated the Treasury's funds, it had to confine itself to executing the latter's instructions. Within its narrow scope it is known to have done its utmost to pursue orthodox lines in its tactics. Indeed, the handling of the official control indicates a degree of orthodoxy which can hardly be attributed to the Treasury. In the long run, however, the Treasury has always had its way. Such is the degree of its control over the Bank of England in practice, if not in law, that it was remarked recently that the nationalisation of the Bank would hardly make any perceptible difference. Although the Bank of England is still owned by its stockholders, for all purposes that matter it is a Government Department. It is true that from time to time it tries to assert itself, and relations with the Treasury are not always ideally smooth, but then such frictions also occur between Government Departments, and the fact that on rare occasions the Bank of England scores on minor issues, does not in any way alter its status which is one of dependence upon the Treasury.

### (5) CONTINENTAL CENTRAL BANKS

The defeat of independent Central Banking was even more sweeping in various continental countries. The efforts to secure the statutory independence of Central Bank Governors failed deplorably during the first months of the crisis. The Governors of the Netherlands Bank, of the Bank of Greece, and of the Austrian National Bank were dismissed at a moment's notice. In the case of Holland and Greece, the cause was the losses suffered on sterling balances, while in Austria

Dr. Reisch was sacrificed to political considerations. In various continental countries Finance Ministers were able to draw freely upon the resources of Central Banks, and if the extent of such inflationary borrowing did not assume a degree comparable with that of the early post-war years, it was simply that the amount of budgetary deficits remained comparatively small. The failure of the idea of independent Central Banking was most evident in the case of Germany. As we said above, to strengthen the independence of the Reichsbank, the Dawes Plan went so far as to establish a certain degree of foreign control over it. After the advent of the National Socialist Government, this foreign control was swept aside and the statutes of the Reichsbank were altered to suit the Government's requirements. It is the irony of fate that Dr. Schacht, the President of the Reichsbank, who at one time was one of the outstanding personalities heading the movement for independent Central Banking, should have been instrumental in his new capacity of Minister of National Economy in passing measures by which the Reichsbank may be compelled to finance public works and to invest its funds in long term bonds.

Even in countries where monetary orthodoxy continues to reign supreme, the orthodox principle of independent Central Banking has been violated. The dismissal of Dr. Vissering by the Dutch Government was one instance proving that independent Central Banking did not survive the crisis even in countries of the Gold Bloc. A much more important and characteristic instance was the recent dismissal of M. Clement Moret, Governor of the Bank of France. Although originally a Treasury official, he was a staunch upholder of the principle of independent Central Banking, and

during 1932–1934 refused on several occasions to grant
accommodation to the French Treasury. As, however,
by the beginning of 1935, the difficulties of covering
the Treasury's requirements threatened to become insurmountable, the Government demanded that the
Bank of France should declare itself willing to rediscount Treasury bills. M. Moret refused to comply
and had to go.

## (6) BANK OF FRANCE'S VICTORY

Much to the surprise of everybody, the Bank of
France put up a remarkable resistance to interference
by M. Flandin's Government. The senior officials did
their best to hinder the adoption of M. Flandin's reflationary policy, their attitude amounting practically to
passive resistance. As for the regents of the Bank,
although they had no actual power, they threatened to
resign and declare in public their objection to the new
policy. In face of such opposition, M. Flandin preferred
not to press his demands. M. Moret's summary dismissal created a bad impression, and it was feared that
the resignation of the regents and the dismissal of the
senior officials might have led to a flight from the franc.
For this reason, M. Flandin preferred to yield and
contented himself with some face-saving devices by
which the Bank of France nominally undertook to
contribute towards the creation of easier monetary
conditions. In reality, the extent to which the new
measures were actually applied was negligible.

Encouraged by this victory, the Bank of France and
the financial circles associated with it took the offensive
in May 1935. Taking advantage of the Treasury's
desperate situation, they dictated the terms on which

they were prepared to assist. They insisted that M.
Flandin should obtain full powers from Parliament to
carry out the unpopular measures required to balance
the Budget. As is well known, both M. Flandin and his
immediate successor, M. Bouisson, failed to obtain
powers from the Chamber, but M. Laval succeeded
where his two predecessors failed. He made use of his
exceptional powers to enforce drastic cuts in order to
balance the Budget.

The victory of the Central Bank over the Government in France was thus complete. If it were to lead
to a fundamental improvement in the French situation
it would undoubtedly strengthen Central Banks against
Governments, not only in France but also in other
countries. In reality, the chances are that the sacrifices
imposed upon the French nation at the insistence of
the Bank of France will merely prolong the agony
without making the least difference to the ultimate
outcome. Thus, in the long run the policy pursued by
the Bank of France will strengthen public opinion
against independent Central Banking both in France
and abroad.

Notwithstanding the temporary victory of the Bank
of France, it is safe to say that the trend of evolution
points towards the decline and disappearance of
independent Central Banking. Nor is the movement, in
the author's opinion, a mere passing phase. It appears
to be in accordance with the general tendency towards
economic planning and increased Government intervention in economic life. The tendency is towards
increasing interference even with private banking and
industrial activities all over Europe. In the circumstances, it is hardly reasonable to expect that Central
Banks should be left undisturbed. Whether or not this

tendency towards increased economic planning will ever be reversed is a question the discussion of which is outside the scope of the present article, but so long as the tendency lasts, it seems bound to manifest itself to a high degree in the sphere of Central Banking.

# CHANGES IN CENTRAL BANK TECHNIQUE AND PRACTICE

## (1) CENTRAL BANKING BEFORE THE WAR

THE tasks with which Central Banks are confronted in these days are totally different from those with which they were faced in the past. Before the war, the monetary system functioned largely automatically and it required a minimum of interference on the part of the monetary authorities. Disturbing tendencies usually carried their own corrective, and the task of Central Banks was confined to assisting to some slight degree the process of automatic readjustment. The exchanges were as a rule allowed to take care of themselves, since the functioning of the gold points kept their fluctuations within narrow limits without any artificial measures on the part of the authorities. In some countries Central Banks pursued a *Devisen-politik* consisting of taking up any excessive supply of foreign exchange during the export season and unloading it during the adverse season. This intervention was, however, too mild in form and in extent to be regarded as a measure of exchange control. The only normal way in which Central Banks sought to influence the exchanges was by the regulation of the bank rate. If they found that they were losing gold too persistently, they raised the bank rate and reduced it again when the pressure was over. Some Central Banks resorted to artificial measures such as paying a premium on gold or paying out silver instead of gold from time to time, but such measures were exceptional. As a rule, the activities of Central Banks consisted of routine work which did not require either imagination or initiative, or even a thorough knowledge of general economic conditions. Anyone acquainted with the technicalities of the money market and who had a good general banking experience was considered to be qualified to run a central bank.

Great Britain in particular was the classical land of the automatic monetary system and of passive Central Banking. The Bank of England managed the monetary affairs of London largely by abstaining from taking action rather than by acting. Its Governor was elected as a matter of routine from among the twenty-six merchant bankers who were directors of the bank, each one of whom was supposed to take his turn as Deputy Governor and Governor. Whether or not he understood anything about monetary policy, he became during two years the supreme guardian of the world's principal currency. What is more, the pre-war Governor of the world's most important Central Bank did not even consider it necessary to resign his partnership in his merchant banking firm while he was in charge of the monetary policy of the country.

Evidently the management of Great Britain's monetary affairs was regarded as a temporary part-time job, which could be safely left to the care of an amateur. Admittedly, more often than not those who became Governors were experienced bankers, well versed in all the details of merchant banking. They would probably have been surprised if anybody had suggested that the management of the monetary affairs of a country required any qualifications other

than those of a perfect merchant banker. It is true
that the Governor was assisted by the permanent
officials of the bank, just as an inexpert Cabinet
Minister is assisted by the highly competent Civil
servants of his Department. But in the majority
of cases these permanent officials were themselves
routine workers with a thorough knowledge of detail
but without any broad vision or any understanding of
the fundamental principles of monetary policy and
Central Banking. That notwithstanding this, the monetary affairs of Great Britain were very well managed
before the war, shows how very little was required
in those days on the part of those who were in charge
of the official monetary policy.

### (2) NEW REQUIREMENTS

Conditions have, however, fundamentally changed
since the war, and more particularly since the crisis.
Without giving a survey of the evolution of Central
Banking during the past twenty years, we will confine
ourselves to registering the changes in the requirements Central Banks have to satisfy. The new requirements can be summarised under the following
headings:

1. Broader vision.
2. More scientific management.
3. More active intervention.
4. More adaptable mentality.

It is no longer sufficient to run a Central Bank
exclusively from the narrow point of view of the
technical monetary situation. Those responsible for
the management of Central Banks have to take into

consideration general conditions outside the financial community. In fact, monetary considerations proper have to be subordinated sometimes to the interests of trade. The opinion expressed by Mr Montagu Norman in his evidence before the Macmillan Committee that in endeavouring to maintain monetary stability, Central Banks serve the interests of industry in the best possible way, is no longer accepted as an axiom of Central Banking.

In the "good old days" it was considered sufficient for Central Banks to watch the figures of their gold reserves and act accordingly. The necessity for scientific methods does not appear to have arisen. Those responsible for the management of Central Banks did not consider it necessary to follow closely tendencies in every sphere of economic activity at home and abroad. Accordingly, most Central Banks had no intelligence department and no statistical department. In the case of the Bank of England, the establishment of a statistical service and general intelligence service dates from only a few years before the crisis. Until recently, it did not even possess adequate statistical records of its own operations.

## (3) ECONOMIC ADVISERS

If it was considered superfluous to acquire an adequate knowledge of current developments there was all the more reason to consider the acquisition of fundamental knowledge unnecessary. Governors and permanent officials of the Bank were in the past, almost without exception, practical men with little or no theoretical knowledge. It was only recently that the Bank of England came to consider it necessary to appoint as economic advisers experts with a thorough theoretical knowledge. While the decision continued to rest with the practical men, at any rate they had the opportunity to obtain the theoretical point of view. The very fact that economic advisers were appointed shows that a knowledge of economics had to be imported from outside, that those in charge of the Bank did not consider themselves adequately equipped. A time will undoubtedly come when an adequate academic background will be considered an indispensable part of the training of a Central Banker. Meanwhile, the appointment of outside advisers is decidedly a step in the right direction.

The need for a more active attitude is by far the most important change in Central Banking practice that has taken place since the war. Before the war, the necessity for active intervention had occasionally arisen in times of crisis. As, however, this only occurred on the average once in seven or eight years, it was the exception and not the rule. Since the war, abnormal conditions necessitating active intervention have become the rule, and relatively calm conditions, when the activity of Central Banks could be confined to routine work, have become the exception. Open market operations have been adopted by practically all Central Banks as part of their routine. Thus, the Central Bank, instead of waiting for the market to approach it, often goes out of its way to influence the market by direct operations.

## (4) EXCHANGE MANAGEMENT

A much more revolutionary innovation has been the active interest taken by monetary authorities in the management of the exchanges. The idea that exchanges can be allowed to take care of themselves has been discarded completely since the crisis, and every country has established a more or less elaborate system of exchange control in which Central Banks have played an important part. Intervention in the foreign exchange market has been carried out by the Central Banks even though in many cases they have operated as mere agents for the Treasuries. Where exchange restrictions have been in operation, they have been handled mostly by the Central Banks. As a result of the active interest taken in the foreign exchange market, the Bank of England, and other Central Banks which in the olden days did not possess foreign exchange departments, have had to create them.

Central Banks have also begun to take a more active part in gold arbitrage. In pre-war days it was carried out almost exclusively by private arbitrageurs, but during the last few years it has become the practice of most Central Banks to import, export, earmark or unearmark gold on their own initiative. In fact, in some countries international gold transactions are carried out exclusively on the initiative of the monetary authorities. In Italy, for instance, no private gold arbitrage is allowed. In Belgium and Switzerland arbitrageurs are at liberty to sell gold to the Central Bank but they cannot withdraw gold. Such export of gold as is necessary for maintaining the stability of the currency is carried out by the Central Banks themselves. Central Banks are also buyers of gold in the open market in London. When during the years before the crisis it was announced that gold was acquired by an "unknown buyer", in most cases the buyer was one of the foreign Central Banks. Since the suspension of

F

the gold standard, the Bank of England and the
Federal Reserve Bank of New York have also been
withdrawing gold from time to time from the Bank of
France, but only for the accounts of their respective
Treasuries who were acting as agents for their re-
spective exchange equalisation funds.

In countries where exchange restrictions exist and
importers have to apply for permits in order to be able
to pay for goods purchased abroad, Central Banks
have assumed the rôle of controllers of imports. The
Reichsbank or the Bank of Italy, for instance, have to
decide whether or not exchange should be allotted
for the import of certain kinds of goods, though in
performing this function they have to follow the rules
laid down by their Governments. In countries with
exchange restrictions, the clerical work attached to
Central Banking has increased immensely, especially
if the Central Banks are in charge of the exchange
clearing accounts.

## (5) CREATED ADAPTABILITY

Among the new requirements of Central Banking,
the possession of an adaptable mentality on the part
of the Board and the Executive of the Central Bank
has become highly essential. The situation has changed
considerably since the war, and what is worse, keeps
on changing frequently and at times unexpectedly.
Central Bankers are confronted from time to time with
sudden changes and have to cope with unforeseen
emergencies. In such circumstances the Central Banker
of the type suited to pre-war requirements would be
unable to fulfil his function satisfactorily. It is no
longer sufficient for the senior officials of a Central

Bank to have picked up a thorough knowledge of technical details during lifelong experience. Indeed, in many ways experience acquired in totally different conditions is a handicap, since it tends to induce the Central Banker to view the present situation with pre-war, or at any rate pre-crisis, eyes. For this reason, the Bank of England and other Central Banks have during the last few years secured the services of young men, who, while possessing little or no previous banking experience, have given evidence of a sufficient degree of initiative and imagination to make up in this respect for the deficiencies of the experienced senior officials.

The new technique of Central Banking is still in its initial stage of development. Nobody knows how much of the practice adopted recently under the pressure of emergency will remain in force and how much of the orthodox practice which ceased to operate will return after the depression has passed. It may be taken for granted, however, that in future Central Banks will remain a much more active factor in the monetary system than in the past. Whether or not they come under the guidance of Treasuries, they will not confine themselves to supervising the automatic working of the system.

# THE FUTURE OF THE BANK FOR INTERNATIONAL SETTLEMENTS

## (1) ORIGINAL OBJECTS OF THE BANK

WHEN in 1930 the Bank for International Settlements was established, some of those responsible for its creation had sanguine hopes of its prospects. Their optimism was shared by the majority of expert opinion, while the general public, in so far as it took an interest in the innovation, regarded it as an important step in the right direction. It was widely believed by experts and laymen alike that the establishment of the Bank for International Settlements marked the opening of a new era in international finance. While in some banking quarters fears were entertained that the new institution might become a dangerous rival to existing banks, generally speaking, its establishment was hailed as a welcome event.

The object of the Bank for International Settlements was twofold. In the first place, it was to facilitate the payment of reparations by Germany on the basis of the Young Plan. Secondly, it was to act as a central organisation to facilitate co-operation between Central Banks. There was a close connection between these two functions. It was evident that co-operation between Central Banks was essential in order to secure the working of the Young Plan. It was less evident at the time, but it became obvious in the light of subsequent events, that developments which led to a breakdown of reparations would inevitably result in a setback to the movement for co-operation between Central Banks.

With our knowledge to-day we may find it difficult to understand how the financiers responsible for the Young Report and the statesmen responsible for The Hague Agreement of 1930 could possibly have been so optimistic as to expect that the mere existence of an international bank could enable Germany to make the huge payments expected of her under the Young Plan. But those idealists who conceived the bank hoped that it would be able to raise world prices and to expand world trade to a sufficient degree to enable Germany to make the transfers which in the existing conditions were evidently far beyond her capacity. These hopes were based on several assumptions which failed to materialise. Firstly, it was assumed that the Central Banks participating in the Bank for International Settlements and the Governments behind them would co-operate whole-heartedly and without any afterthought in order to attain a common end. It was equally assumed that the bank would have a fair chance to develop and that its early period of development would not be interrupted by a crisis of exceptional gravity. Lastly, it was assumed that those responsible for governing the destinies of the bank would be inspired by the same ambitious and enterprising spirit as inspired the originators of the scheme. Each of these assumptions proved unfounded.

## (2) NO ADEQUATE CO-OPERATION

The anticipation that the Bank for International Settlements would be managed in a spirit of genuine co-operation between the monetary authorities of the

leading countries failed to materialise. Indeed, it required an unusual degree of optimism to expect that
the mere establishment of that bank would eliminate
the fundamental disagreement on policy that existed
between nations. Had there been an agreement that
it was desirable to use the facilities provided by the
bank to bring about a considerable rise in world prices,
the experience of the early period of the bank might
have provided ɩ fair test of its possibilities. As it is,
we are not entitled to conclude that the bank is not
suitable to achieve such an end. All we are entitled to
say is that in the absence of agreement as to the end
the bank should pursue, it is bound to be useless as an
instrument of international monetary policy.

But even if there had been genuine co-operation
between the leading countries, it is doubtful whether
the bank could have produced spectacular results
within the very short time of its existence prior to
the financial crisis of 1931. Its early development
was bound to be slow. Given the fact that the bank
was established in May 1930, and that exactly twelve
months later an international banking crisis that shook
the world to its foundations broke loose, it can hardly
be said that the bank had a fair chance to get over the
initial stage of its development.

Last but by no means least, the bank was handicapped during the early period of its existence by the
highly conservative character of the institutions that
controlled its destinies. The Central Banks represented
on its Board of Directors were ultra-orthodox organisations, hostile to the idea of experimenting, of rapid
expansion, and of taking any risk incompatible with
Central Banking principles and traditions. Month
after month, suggestions were put forward at the

Board meetings at Basle to expand the bank's sphere of activity. These proposals, however useful they may have appeared to be, were rejected by the Board of Directors. "If in doubt, do nothing" is a time-honoured slogan which has been applied persistently throughout the five years' existence of the bank. As it is less risky to say "no" than to say "yes", those in charge of the bank have preferred to be on the safe side by abstaining from what they considered bold innovations.

Nor did the hopes that the bank would stimulate friendly collaboration between Central Banks materialise. The atmosphere at the monthly board meetings was anything but cordial during 1930 and 1931, and at times these meetings witnessed violent clashes between conflicting interests. Indeed, it was suggested that these meetings were, if anything, harmful to international co-operation, since they provided an opportunity for clashes which might have been avoided but for the necessity for the Central Bank Governors to meet once a month.

### (3) BANK HELPLESS AGAINST CRISIS

Within the limited means at its disposal, the Bank for International Settlements made an effort to avert the financial crisis. It granted substantial credits to the Central Banks of Germany, Austria, Hungary, and Jugoslavia. It did not, however, possess the means required for intervention on a sufficiently large scale to prevent the crisis. Had the crisis taken place in, say, 1941 instead of 1931, it is conceivable that in the meantime the bank might have accumulated funds running into milliards, in which case it might have been in a better position to intervene effectively. As it was, the crisis simply immobilised the bank's relatively moderate resources and rendered it incapable of granting any further assistance. Indeed, whatever liquid resources it possessed were withdrawn by the Central Banks which kept deposits with it. Whenever a frozen loan was repaid, there was a corresponding withdrawal of deposits so that the liquid funds of the bank have been negligible since May 1931.

It was evident that after 1931 the bank could no longer attempt to influence the course of events. Notwithstanding this, its passive attitude during the years of depression deserves criticism. The fact that it could not hope to achieve results of fundamental importance did not justify its utter inactivity between 1931 and 1935. There were ample opportunities for rendering useful services and there was no lack of interesting suggestions. Indeed, the Executive of the bank, anxious to earn its keep, was fertile in producing and putting forward new and interesting ideas. The Board of Directors invariably rejected them, however, or instituted prolonged and futile enquiries into them as a preliminary to their rejection. Beyond an attempt to establish international postal clearing, nothing was done that could be quoted on the credit side of the bank's balance-sheet of activity since the beginning of the crisis.

Evidently the Directors made no efforts to justify the existence of the bank. Indeed, they appeared to be under the impression that the mere fact that the monthly board meetings provided an opportunity for them to meet, was in itself a sufficient justification for the existence of the institution. They failed to realise that the bank's prolonged inactivity was undermining the initial authority it possessed. From time to time they issued ponderous manifestoes from Basle laying down the law as to the monetary policy the Governments should pursue. Had the bank been more active in helping the world to work out its salvation, the voice of its Board would have carried considerable weight. As it was, Governments and public opinion could hardly be blamed for ignoring the unsolicited advice they received from time to time from Basle. There was in fact only one piece of advice the Directors of the Bank for International Settlements were anxious to give and that was that every country should return to the gold standard as soon as possible. But they did not even trouble to work out practical proposals as to how this end could best be achieved.

The bank has thus proved to be a disappointment, not because it was unable to prevent the crisis but because it failed to make an effort to make itself useful during the period of depression. The world gradually lost interest in the institution which in its present form is barely more than a club for Central Bank Governors.

### (4) ATTITUDE TOWARDS STABILISATION

Will the bank ever be able to develop into something more than it is at present? Most of its Directors would answer that once the world has returned to the gold standard the future of the bank is assured. They are not particularly concerned with the circumstances of stabilisation so long as it is done quickly. They would like the world to stabilise first and to think of the consequences afterwards. Fortunately, the Governments on whom the responsibility for the act of stabilisation would rest are not so keen to undertake for a second time a leap in the dark. Whatever the reasons

for and against stabilisation, no country is likely to
stabilise merely in order to enable the Bank for International Settlements to expand and consolidate its
position. Indeed, it would be a grave mistake from the
point of view of the prospects of the bank itself if the
Governments were to return to the gold standard prematurely and unconditionally. Having attained what
they wanted, the Central Bank Governors would then
continue their policy of declining to undertake anything in the way of reform and the bank would remain
in all probability what it now is. Its resources and
activities might expand to some extent, but it would
never be able to play a rôle of first-rate importance in
the sphere of international finance.

In order to induce the bank to take a more active
part, the Governments will have to play on its intense
desire for a return to the gold standard by making
stabilisation conditional upon certain reforms the
execution of which must be undertaken by the bank.
This is not the place to discuss in detail the exact form
the future gold standard should assume, but it is
certain that the Bank for International Settlements
ought to play an important part in securing its normal
functioning.

It is not the popular suggestion of an international
gold reserve that we have in mind. The chances of this
suggestion materialising are now probably much less
favourable than they were before the crisis. Owing to
the increase of economic nationalism and political
tension on the Continent since 1931, it is unthinkable
that any country would consider it desirable to keep
the larger part of its gold reserve abroad. There is
certainly no question of pooling the gold resources of
various countries. It is unthinkable that France or the

United States would ever consent to such an arrangement. Barring that solution, the whole scheme of transferring gold reserves to the Bank for International Settlements would boil down to technical measures to substitute book entries for gold shipments. This idea has always been very popular in certain quarters on the ground that the shifting of gold from one centre to another is sheer waste. As, however, the amount of waste involved is negligible, it is hardly worth while to reorganise an international monetary system merely for the sake of saving a few hundred thousand pounds a year. Those who attach much importance to this scheme are inclined to mistake the shadow for the substance. What is required is not to reduce the physical movements of gold but to bring under reasonable control the economic and financial tendencies that cause such movements. In this respect, the Bank for International Settlements could play a very useful part, but only if it is not afraid of breaking new ground.

## (5) ATTITUDE TOWARDS EXCHANGE CLEARING

By becoming a clearing-house for international transfers the Bank for International Settlements could play an important part in reducing the disturbing influences which lead to unwanted gold movements. This suggestion has been made in various forms ever since the establishment of the bank, but has been rejected on the ground that it would reduce the volume of foreign exchange business and would thus be detrimental to the banking interests engaged in foreign exchange transactions. Undoubtedly, this is true. The question is whether it would not be worth while to sacrifice these banking interests in order to secure a higher degree of international monetary stability.

The obvious function the Bank for International Settlements should undertake is that of a central clearing-house for international exchange clearing. As is well known, a large number of exchange clearing agreements have been concluded during the last three years, and are operating independently of each other. Thanks to these exchange clearing arrangements countries which have been particularly affected by the crisis have been able to retain a reasonable part of their foreign trade. By enabling the countries of Central and South-eastern Europe to trade with each other and to some extent with stronger countries, the exchange clearing system has probably saved them from utter financial and economic collapse. If the system has been unable to produce wholly satisfactory results it is because there has been a complete lack of co-ordination between the various exchange clearing agreements which have been operating independently of each other. Although in some cases triangular exchange clearing arrangements have been made by which it was possible to use the surplus on one clearing account to offset the deficit on another, such arrangements have been the exception and not the rule. What is wanted is a central organisation which would co-ordinate the working of the various exchange clearing agreements and which would systematically offset surpluses on certain accounts against deficiencies on others.

The Bank for International Settlements is eminently suited to perform this function. It is, therefore, unfortunate that the Board of that bank should have chosen to adopt a hostile attitude towards the system. Not only is the bank unwilling to lend a helping hand in its development, but it is doing its utmost to handicap it. The Central Bank Governors represented on its Board have, in fact, pledged themselves to obstruct the development of exchange clearing. This attitude is deplorable, not only from the point of view of the general interest which would be best served by the rapid development of the system of exchange clearing, but also from the point of view of the Central Banks and the Bank for International Settlements itself. The exchange clearing system is, in our opinion, the rational system for international transfers, and its universal adoption is a mere question of time. If it does not take place as a consequence of the present depression, it will take place after the next crisis. The resistance of Central Banks and of the Bank for International Settlements will be unable to prevent its development. The system will be adopted without them by other organisations, and both Central Banks and the Bank for International Settlements will lose a great deal of their influence. The international monetary system will slip out of their control entirely through their own fault. The future of the Bank for International Settlements depends largely if not exclusively upon its attitude towards exchange clearing. If it continues to work against the system, some other international organisation will have to be formed to take charge of international clearing, and will soon be overshadowing the moribund bank of Basle.

# FOREIGN STERLING BALANCES

## (1) A POPULAR MISCONCEPTION

A GREAT deal has been said in recent years about foreign balances in London. They played a very important part in causing the suspension of the gold standard in 1931, and ever since the attitude of their holders has been a most important factor in determining the fluctuations of sterling. The desire of foreigners to increase their sterling balances, either because they anticipated an appreciation of sterling, or because they distrusted their own currency, has caused from time to time a sharp appreciation, while their desire to reduce their sterling balances, either because they were afraid of a depreciation or because they preferred to transfer their funds to their own country or to some other foreign centre, have been responsible for substantial declines in sterling. Both appreciation and depreciation have been mitigated since 1932 by the operations of the Exchange Equalisation Account.

It is a popular belief that whenever there is a flight to the pound, the total volume of foreign balances in London undergoes a considerable increase, and that whenever there is a flight from the pound there is a slump in the volume of foreign sterling balances. On this assumption, the view is held that the task of the Exchange Equalisation Account is to acquire the counterpart of the increased foreign sterling balances by increasing its own holding of gold or gold exchanges. The idea is that if the authorities acquire an amount of gold equal to the additional foreign deposits coming to London, they will be in a position to repurchase the sterling from foreign holders when the latter become anxious to unload their holdings. This view is widely held both among practical bankers and academic economists. Among the latter, Mr N. F. Hall in his recently published book on *The Exchange Equalisation Account* based his whole conception of the working of the Exchange Equalisation Account on this view. In his opinion it is the duty of the authorities to endeavour to adjust the amount of gold and foreign currencies they acquire to the amount of sterling balances acquired by foreign holders.

## (2) EFFECT OF FOREIGN BUYING AND SELLING

In reality, the popular conception about the circumstances of the increase and decrease in foreign balances is entirely erroneous. On repeated occasions when there was evidence of heavy buying or selling pressure on sterling, the author was told by leading bankers who were in a position to know that the total of their foreign balances had remained practically unaffected by the movement. Contrary to what they would have considered natural, the buying pressure of foreigners did not cause a sharp rise, or their selling pressure a sharp fall, in foreign deposits. They were puzzled by this, and were at a loss to explain it. To give a concrete example, during the fall of sterling in March 1935, bankers were unanimous in asserting that there was no appreciable decline in their foreign deposits. Since there was no evidence of any substantial speculative selling of sterling, nor of any substantial change in foreign holdings on sterling

securities, they were completely at a loss to explain the
selling pressure. And yet the explanation was simple.
In a country off the gold standard, there is no need
whatever for buying and selling pressure on the currency to bring about a rise or a fall in foreign balances.

Under the gold standard, a heavy buying pressure
on sterling results in its appreciation above gold
import point and the counterpart of an increase of
foreign deposits is thus provided by an influx of gold.
Conversely, if there is heavy selling of sterling, the
result is a depreciation below gold export point and
the counterpart of the decrease of the total of foreign
balances is thus provided by an efflux of gold. After
the suspension of the gold standard, however, gold
movements ceased to provide automatically the
counterpart of fluctuations in the total foreign capital
held in London. Although it is possible to buy and
sell fairly large quantities of gold in the London
market, since the market price moves in sympathy
with the gold exchanges, there is no reason why a
depreciation of sterling should result in an efflux
or an appreciation in an influx. The movement
of gold between the London market and foreign
centres is determined by totally different considerations.

### (3) RÔLE OF EXCHANGE EQUALISATION ACCOUNT

In the circumstances, assuming that the balance of
payments is neutral, the only way in which foreigners
can increase their sterling balances is if they are able
to find somebody, British or foreign, prepared to sell
sterling to them. The only way in which foreigners
can reduce their sterling balances is by finding some-

body, British or foreign, to buy sterling from them. British buyers or sellers may be either private firms and individuals or the Exchange Equalisation Account. It is a well-known fact that British firms and individuals are not as a rule in the habit of keeping large foreign balances and do not speculate in foreign exchanges on a large scale. The chances are that, when there is a buying pressure on sterling, foreign potential buyers do not easily find British private sellers. This means that, unless the Exchange Equalisation Account is prepared to sell sterling, they will have to find some foreign holders willing to sell—at a price. Conversely, when there is a selling pressure on sterling, the chances are that foreign holders will not easily find British firms or individuals willing to take over their holdings. Unless the Exchange Equalisation Account is prepared to buy the sterling from them, they will have to find other foreigners who are prepared to acquire sterling at a price. This means that, unless the Exchange Equalisation Account operates, the predominant majority of transactions in sterling during a buying or selling pressure take place between foreigners. Both buyers and sellers are mostly foreigners, and there is no reason why the total of foreign balances in London should change at all. Individual holdings may change hands any number of times but remain in foreign possession.

This explains why during the fall in sterling in March 1935 the total foreign balances in London showed no decline. Foreign holders anxious to sell had to find foreign buyers by reducing the exchange rate at which they were prepared to sell. There was selling pressure and the rate fell, but the volume of foreign holdings remained unchanged.

G

Had the Exchange Equalisation Account intervened to support sterling on a large scale, the state of affairs would have been totally different. In that case foreign holders of balances in London would have sold their sterling to the Exchange Equalisation Account and their total holding would thus have declined. It is only if the Exchange Equalisation Account operates on a large scale that the total of foreign balances in London is affected to a noteworthy extent. If the Exchange Equalisation Account buys sterling in order to prevent its depreciation, the total declines. If the Exchange Equalisation Account sells sterling in order to prevent an unwanted appreciation the total increases.

### (4) CAUSE OR EFFECT?

Evidently the operations of the Exchange Equalisation Account constitute a cause and not a consequence of the changes in the total volume of foreign balances in London. It is not correct to say that the operations of the Exchange Equalisation Account have been made necessary by the increase or the decrease of foreign balances. On the contrary, what actually happens is that such increases or decreases cannot take place unless and until the Exchange Equalisation Account operates. This assumes, of course, that the balance of payments is in equilibrium. If there is an import surplus foreign balances will naturally tend to increase, while an export surplus will tend to reduce the total of foreign holdings. In a similar way, if gold is imported and sold in the London market it will tend to increase the total amount of foreign balances, provided that the buyers of gold, whether British or foreign, possess already the sterling required and need not have to buy it from another foreign holder. The increase in overseas balances in London during the last three years or so has been largely due to the sale of Indian and South African gold.

Barring an import surplus, whether it consists of gold or commodities, the only way in which foreign balances in London can materially increase is through sales of sterling by the Exchange Equalisation Account. Barring an export surplus, the only way in which foreign balances in London can materially decline is through the purchase of sterling by the Exchange Equalisation Account. It is essential to bear these facts in mind in order to understand the situation. Once we are aware of this, we must also realise that the task of the Exchange Equalisation Account does not consist in acquiring gold and foreign exchange to an equivalent of the increase in the foreign sterling balances. But for its intervention, there would be no increase. The reason why the Exchange Equalisation Account acquires foreign balances when there is a buying pressure on sterling is not because it is desirous to hold the counterpart of the foreign sterling balances, but because it desires to prevent an unwanted appreciation of sterling. It is unable to do so without causing an increase in foreign balances by means of its purchases of gold and foreign exchanges. The result is that, simultaneously with the increase of the Exchange Equalisation Account's gold holdings, there is also an increase in foreign sterling balances as an inevitable consequence of the measures taken to prevent a rise in sterling.

When there is a selling pressure on sterling, the

Exchange Equalisation Account sells gold and exchanges, not in order to keep pace with the outflow of foreign balances but in order to prevent an unwanted depreciation of sterling. The decline in foreign balances is merely an inevitable consequence of the operations of the Exchange Equalisation Account. But for these operations, foreign holders desiring to get rid of their sterling would have to find some other foreign purchaser.

It is reasonable to assume that, in formulating the policy of the Exchange Equalisation Account, the British authorities are guided largely if not exclusively by the tendency of the exchange rates. Changes in the amount of foreign balances cannot serve as a guide to their policy, since it is they themselves who determine that tendency by means of the operations of the Equalisation Account.

## (5) RESOURCES OF EXCHANGE EQUALISATION ACCOUNT

It would be a mistake to infer from what we said above that since the amount of foreign balances is largely determined by the operations of the Exchange Equalisation Account, and since there can be no increase unless the Exchange Equalisation Account buys a corresponding amount of gold, it necessarily possesses gold assets equivalent to the foreign balances held in London. In the first place, there were already substantial foreign balances at the time of the suspension of the gold standard which possessed no equivalent in the form of gold assets. Moreover, the equivalent of £130 million (gold) of foreign sterling balances that was transferred to this country at the end of 1931 and in the beginning of 1932 was used up for the repayment of the Franco-American credits. In addition, the Exchange Equalisation Account sold the Bank of England a sum of over £60 million (gold) worth of gold, so that, roughly speaking, it has a deficiency of £200 million (gold) compared with the foreign balances in addition to the amount of the balances which were already here on September 21, 1931. It is true that these £200 million are covered by the Bank of England's gold holding, but this reserve is not available so long as this country keeps off the gold standard. In any case, the balances that existed on September 21, 1931, are largely uncovered. The only item that could be offset against them is the appreciation of the gold reserve both of the Bank of England and of the Exchange Equalisation Account in terms of sterling. Considerable as this appreciation has been, it must certainly fall short of the amount of the surplus of foreign balances.

The only way in which this deficiency could possibly be covered would be by allowing sterling to depreciate further. As a result of its depreciation, the sterling amount of foreign sterling balances would of course remain unchanged, while the sterling equivalent of the gold holdings of the Bank of England and the Exchange Equalisation Account would increase. If the depreciation were to go much further, the result would be a net surplus of the combined gold reserve over the short-term liabilities to foreign countries. There are, of course, on the other side of the balance-sheet the short-term assets represented by banking credits to foreign borrowers. The greater part of these credits, however, is frozen and cannot, therefore, be reckoned as a counterpart to the short-term liabilities.

# THE LONDON GOLD MARKET

## (1) CONDITIONS BEFORE THE CRISIS

WHILE Great Britain was on the gold standard, the London gold market was of secondary importance from a monetary point of view. The whole organisation merely provided technical facilities for disposing of the newly produced gold and of such other consignments as were occasionally realised by holders. Its scope was narrow and its activities simple. The fact that the Bank of England was prepared to buy gold to an unlimited amount at the price of 84s. 10d. per ounce, and that it was prepared to sell gold to an unlimited amount at the price of 84s. 11½d. per ounce, restricted the range of possible fluctuations in the market to within those two figures. There was no forward dealing and almost all the business was done at the official fixing that took place every day at 11 A.M. The gold market had only one really active day each week. The South African mail-boat arrived on Mondays and its gold consignment, which constituted by far the largest part of the gold handled in the London market, was disposed of on Tuesdays. For the rest of the week there was as a rule very little business in gold and the daily quotation was very frequently nominal.

The whole organisation and activities of the gold market prior to 1931 were of very little interest to the student of monetary problems. To some extent the existence of a gold market in London favoured the Bank of England, since it had the first call on the world's newly produced gold. As, however, an excessive increase in the bank's gold reserve would have produced its own corrective by its effect on sterling, the advantage was more apparent than real. To some extent the open market played the part of a shock absorber, since it diverted gold transactions which would otherwise have affected the reserve of the Bank of England. To a very large extent, however, the same result would have been achieved if dealings in gold had not been concentrated in London, and if producers had sold their output directly to the Central Banks, which acquired it eventually through the intermediary of the London market. It may be said that the existence of an open market for gold in London did not in any way influence British monetary policy. From the point of view of monetary problems it was, therefore, a *quantité négligeable*.

## (2) CHANGES SINCE THE CRISIS

This state of affairs has undergone a fundamental change since the suspension of the gold standard. The London gold market has become a factor of first-rate importance in the international monetary sphere. The student of monetary questions can no longer afford to ignore it. Under the changed conditions it has conferred upon the British monetary system a unique status among the world's monetary systems. Owing to the possession of an open market for gold with a large turnover, Great Britain occupies a position somewhere half-way between the countries on a gold basis and those with an inconvertible currency. For although Great Britain suspended the gold standard on September 21, 1931, the pound sterling never for a moment

ceased to be convertible into gold. In other countries
which suspended the gold standard, holders of notes
ceased to be in a position to acquire gold in a legitimate
way, and their facilities for acquiring gold illegitimately
were limited. In Great Britain, thanks to the existence
of an open market in gold free of restrictions, everybody was at liberty to exchange their notes for gold.
All that happened was that the notes ceased to be convertible into gold at a fixed parity. They could be
converted, however, to an unlimited extent at the
current market price. Indeed, it may be said that
Great Britain adopted a new monetary system, a
kind of elastic gold standard in which notes remained
convertible into gold and the export of gold remained
free, and which differed from the orthodox gold standard only in that the gold parity was elastic instead of
being rigid.

The mere fact that there was an open market for gold
in London, which was allowed to exercise its function
without the legal restrictions customary in countries
which had suspended the gold standard, would not in
itself have justified this interpretation of the new monetary situation in Great Britain. Had the facilities of the
London gold market remained approximately the same
as before the suspension of the gold standard, it would
not have assumed this significance from a monetary
point of view. For before 1931 the facilities provided
by the London gold market were by no means unlimited. As often as not, buyers were only able to
satisfy their requirements on one day during the week,
and even a most persistent demand would not have
resulted in an increase in the supply. Sellers were in a
better position to dispose of their stocks, but this was
only because between 1925 and 1931 there happened

to be a persistent monetary demand for gold. At present, however, the London gold market is in a position to satisfy any requirements and to absorb any supply. Although there is no official seller bound by statutes to sell on demand an unlimited amount of gold, the supply in the open market is practically unlimited. Although there is no official buyer bound by law to take over at a fixed price any supplies which no one else wants, the open market is in a position to absorb a practically unlimited quantity of gold.

## (3) INCREASED TURNOVER

The actual supplies of the London market are plentiful and its potential supplies immense. In addition to the newly mined gold which continues to arrive, regularly, there is also a regular flow of gold to the market from India and other countries engaged in dishoarding. What is even more important from the point of view of continuity of supply, there are at present in London huge private holdings of gold acquired for the purpose of hoarding, speculation, or arbitrage. Estimates of the amount of privately owned gold in London vary widely, the most conservative figure being £200 million. A very large proportion of this constitutes the reserve the market can draw upon. It is true that many holders keep gold in London merely as a means to avoid capital depreciation and that such deposits hardly ever change hands.

There are, however, other holders who acquire and hold gold in London for speculative purposes and are prepared to realise their stocks if the price offered is sufficiently attractive. Another by no means inconsiderable portion of the privately owned gold stocks

in London serves the purpose of covering certain
exchange risks, or, thanks to the development of a
forward market in gold, provides facilities for earning a comparatively high rate of interest on liquid
funds. These categories of gold deposits change hands
frequently and contribute towards keeping up a large
and regular turnover which secures the efficiency of
the London gold market. Indeed, the amount of gold
that changed hands during 1934 at the daily official
fixing alone was about £124 million, an average of
over £400,000 per working day, which is very much in
excess of the amount dealt with before the war or
before the suspension of the gold standard. Moreover,
since 1931 the practice has developed of dealing in gold
on a large scale throughout the day. The amount of
spot and forward gold transactions carried out in the
unofficial market is frequently larger than the amount
dealt with at the official fixing. No statistics are available about the turnover in the unofficial market, but it
is certain that the total dealt with in London as a
whole is now several times larger than before the
suspension of the gold standard.

In addition to its regular supplies, the London
market can also draw on the reserves of the Bank of
France, provided that the price is sufficiently attractive. While the other countries of the Gold Bloc and
the United States do not allow gold to be withdrawn
for sale in London, France has not, up to now, raised
any objection to such transactions. Thus, if there
is a persistent demand which cannot be satisfied
in the market, a rise in the price of gold can always
attract a sufficient amount from Paris to make up for
the deficiency. It is true that before 1931 gold was
shipped by arbitrageurs from the various Central

Banks for sale in London. The difficulty of such operations was that before the crisis the London market was confined to spot transactions in gold actually in London. The mere fact that the open market price for gold was above the statutory buying price of the Bank of England did not always attract shipments from foreign Central Banks, since arbitrageurs would have had to have run the risk of finding no buyers at the higher price and of being forced to sell the gold eventually at a loss to the Bank of England. The situation is totally different at present. Gold is now transacted for forward delivery, and there are any number of holders with stocks in London prepared to sell at an attractive price and replenish their holdings immediately from the Bank of France.

If the supply of gold in the London market is practically unlimited, so is the demand. In addition to the demand for private hoarding, which fluctuates widely, there is the demand for speculation, for hedging against exchange losses, and for the employment of liquid funds. There is also buying on behalf of foreign Central Banks, and there is strong reason to believe that on occasion the Exchange Equalisation Fund and its American equivalent enter the market. If all this demand is unable to absorb the supply, the price of gold tends to fall sufficiently to make it profitable to ship gold from London for sale to the Bank of France or to the monetary authorities of a number of other countries, which, while unwilling to sell gold to the London market, are quite prepared to receive gold consigned to them from London by arbitrageurs.

## (4) FREEDOM OF THE MARKET

Apart from the increase in the turnover and the greater elasticity of supply and demand in the London gold market, its rise into prominence has also been due to the freedom from legal interference or moral pressure to which would-be purchasers of gold are exposed in other countries. After the suspension of the gold standard, the legal status of the gold market remained unchanged. As before, everybody was at liberty to buy or sell gold in unlimited amounts at any price, to hold it in this country, or to have it shipped abroad. Other countries when suspending the gold standard imposed restrictions on the acquisition and holding of gold by private interests. Some countries went so far as to compel holders to surrender their gold stock against the payment of the statutory buying price of the monetary authorities. In Great Britain the only limitation of this kind is the right of the Bank of England under the Currency and Bank Notes Act of 1928 to compel holders resident in this country to surrender their holding in excess of £10,000 against the payment of the statutory selling price. Even this restriction has not been made use of except in the case of gold held by British banks. In any case, it already existed before the suspension of the gold standard. As for foreign holders, their freedom is as complete as in any country on an effective gold standard. British subjects are of course also entitled to buy gold in unlimited amounts for the purpose of exporting it; and to import gold for sale to foreigners without running the risk of being compelled to surrender it at a lower price. Regarding the legal position, the situation in Great Britain is much more similar to that of a country on a gold basis than to that of a country with an inconvertible currency.

### (5) IMPROVED TECHNICAL FACILITIES

The technical facilities of the London gold market have improved considerably since 1931. It was only after the suspension of the gold standard that dealings in forward gold developed. Strictly speaking, this development is not altogether new. In the East there have always been fairly active local forward markets for gold, both in India and China. In London itself there had already been forward transactions before the crisis. In particular, during the period of weakness of sterling towards the end of 1930 and the beginning of 1931, the practice was adopted of buying the South African gold production before it had reached the London market. As soon as the gold left the Johannesburg refinery it was bought forward. The reason for this was the peculiar situation that arose from the Bank of England's decision to pay out gold of standard fineness only and the decision of the Bank of France to accept gold of 0·996 fineness only. It was necessary, in consequence, to have the gold bars withdrawn from the Bank of England refined before delivering them to the Bank of France. As the refining facilities available both in London and Paris fell short of requirements, it was impossible to ship to Paris a sufficient amount of gold to offset the selling pressure on sterling. The result was a depreciation of sterling below the gold export point. This caused uneasiness amongst French holders of sterling balances, some of whom sought to cover themselves by acquiring gold for later delivery. As the Bank of England itself was not prepared to undertake the forward sale of gold, they bought forward the South African gold output. When this peculiar situation came to an end early in 1931 through the decision of the Bank of France to accept bar gold of standard fineness, the practice of buying gold for forward delivery was also discontinued.

After the suspension of the gold standard in Great Britain, regular forward dealing in gold gradually developed. The practice is not officially recognised, and when the bullion brokers fix the daily official price of gold they only transact business in gold for spot delivery. Unofficially, however, there is fairly active dealing in forward gold; there are days when many hundreds of thousands of pounds change hands.

Forward gold is always at a premium against spot gold, but the premium fluctuates: usually it is between 10d. and 1s. 2d. for three months and 2s. 2d. to 2s. 5d. for six months. At these rates it secures an adequate yield to holders of gold who are prepared to sell their holdings forward, after allowing for the expenses that attach to keeping gold deposited during three months. Those who possess facilities of their own for the purpose can earn over 3 per cent per annum on the capital engaged in such transactions.

### (6) FORWARD GOLD DEALINGS

Among the buyers of forward gold are speculators who expect that sterling will depreciate and the price of gold rise in consequence. It may be asked why such speculators do not buy forward francs or forward dollars instead of forward gold. The premium on forward francs is much lower than the premium on forward gold, while forward dollars can be acquired at a discount. If, in spite of this, they are prepared to pay the relatively high premium on gold, it is because in buying forward francs or dollars they expose themselves to the risk of a depreciation of those two currencies in terms of gold, in addition to the risk of an appreciation of sterling; while if they buy forward gold they are only exposed to the risk of an appreciation of sterling. Another purpose for which gold is bought forward is to secure residents in the countries of the Gold Bloc against a devaluation of their national currencies. The same object can be achieved, of course, at a much lower cost by buying spot gold and keeping it on deposit in London. In many cases, however, those desirous of safeguarding themselves against a devaluation of their currencies are not in a position to immobilise their capital for any length of time; or possibly they earn a yield on their capital in excess of the cost of the forward gold operation. Let us suppose, for instance, that a Swiss capitalist wants to safeguard his capital, tied up in Swiss securities, against a depreciation of the Swiss franc. To that end, he has to sell Swiss francs forward, and at the same time buy gold forward for the same period. If, before the contracts mature, the franc depreciates in terms of gold, he will have the full benefit of the rise of gold in terms of Swiss francs. By merely selling Swiss francs forward against sterling, he might obtain the same profit, but he is exposed to the risk of a depreciation of sterling in terms of Swiss francs. If, however, the transaction is combined with a forward purchase of gold, he is safeguarded against that risk.

Gold is also bought forward for the purpose of hedging operations by British speculators in Wall Street and other foreign markets. Needless to say, the hedging

is far from watertight, for an appreciation of sterling
and a fall in the sterling price of gold might easily
inflict loss upon them.

Sellers of forward gold are, in the first place, holders
of gold anxious to earn interest; as the risk involved
in selling gold forward is very small, provided that the
deal is done with the right people, it is a profitable
line of activity. Speculators who anticipate an appreciation of sterling also may find it more convenient to
sell gold forward rather than to contract a short
position in dollars or francs. Forward selling of gold
is also used as a hedge against the depreciation of the
dollar or franc by holders of American or French
securities. Lastly, some holders of gold-mining shares
who want to eliminate the exchange risk can do so by
selling gold forward, even though in taking this course
they also eliminate their chances of benefiting by a
depreciation of sterling.

Thanks to its excellent technical facilities, the elasticity of supply and demand, and its freedom from
legal restrictions, the London gold market has become
from an international point of view something like the
equivalent of Central Banks in countries on a gold
basis. London can be depended upon to cover gold
requirements to the same extent as if the Bank of
England were still under statutory obligation to sell
unlimited amounts. She can be relied upon to absorb
supplies to the same extent as if the Bank of England
were still under statutory obligation to buy unlimited
amounts.

## (7) A SETBACK

The development of the London gold market suffered
a severe setback in June 1935 when an unofficial

embargo was imposed on forward gold transactions of a speculative nature. This step was taken by the Bank of England in order to assist the French authorities in their fight against speculation. Before June 1935 the authorities had already endeavoured to discourage the clearing banks from lending on the security of gold, but on this occasion they went much further in that they approached, directly or indirectly, all sections of the London banking community and requested them to refrain both from lending on gold and from executing forward transactions unless they were satisfied as to their genuine commercial character.

The result of this intervention was a sharp contraction in the volume of forward operations in gold. Needless to say, it was not only the speculative elements that suffered through the restrictions, but genuine trade was also penalised. In order to be able to do forward business for genuine purposes on a large scale, it is necessary to have an active market with a large turnover. More often than not in the past the counterpart for genuine buying or selling of forward gold was provided by speculation. Once speculative operations have been reduced to a minimum through the unofficial embargo, it becomes much more difficult to find a counterpart for genuine purposes. The authorities in trying to prevent speculation in gold have thus managed to deal a severe blow at the legitimate facilities offered by the London gold market.

It remains to be seen whether the effect on speculation in francs was worth the sacrifice. Judging by the experience of the run on the Dutch guilder in July 1935, the answer is in the negative. Since the Dutch had no facilities for buying forward gold in London, they resorted to withdrawing gold from the Nether-

H

lands Bank on a much larger scale than ever before. A loss of some £20 million of gold in one single week is an experience without precedent in the history of the Netherlands Bank. It is reasonable to assume that the Bank of France will have a similar experience when the next run on the franc occurs. The London forward market acted to a very large extent as a shock absorber for Central Banks on a gold basis, and its destruction was a short-sighted act which has benefited nobody. From the point of view of London's development as a world banking centre, it was a retrograde step. It wiped out one of the few advantages gained from the crisis which would otherwise have compensated London for the loss of some of her international business.

# SIGNOR MUSSOLINI'S DILEMMA

## (1) INTRODUCTORY

THE rôle of a dictator is in many ways far from enviable. It is true that he can concentrate in his hands all the power which in democratic countries is shared by the members of the Cabinet, Parliament, and the electorate. He has, however, to pay the price for his exceptional freedom of action in the form of an immense responsibility which he has to carry unaided. It is true that in taking his decisions he can disregard the opinions, interests, and feelings of his Cabinet Ministers, of the members of the various councils that may survive as the remains of the defunct Parliamentary system, and, to a large degree, of the general public. But exactly because his decisions escape the modifying influence and criticism of these factors, he must at times feel the burden of his immense responsibility to a larger extent than any Prime Minister or head of a State under Parliamentary democracy.

Signor Mussolini provides an example of the dictator who is well aware of the burden of his responsibility. This burden is heavier even than that of the immense amount of work he has been doing during the last thirteen years. Although he is in charge of some seven Government Departments, and takes an active interest in practically everything of importance that happens in Italy, he stands the strain very well. He seems to possess an amazing capacity for work, for grasping the substance of problems within the shortest

possible time, and for finding time for everything that
he considers important. It is not the volume of work
that is weighing upon him, but the immense responsibility he has to carry. And the author believes he is
not far wrong in assuming that among all the problems
with which Signor Mussolini has been confronted, the
monetary dilemma is the one which has been worrying
him the most.

### (2) THE MISTAKE OF 1926

On August 26, 1926, Signor Mussolini declared in a
speech delivered at Pesaro, "We shall defend the lira
to the last drop of our blood". Ever since, this declaration has formed the basis of his whole monetary
policy and to a very large extent of his whole economic
policy. The immediate consequence of his statement
was a sharp appreciation of the lira, which was stabilised in the following year at too high a level. The
result was that Italy underwent a period of economic
depression at a time when the rest of the world was
enjoying prosperity. The economic depression began
in Italy in 1926 instead of in 1930. As a result, in 1931,
when the world as a whole found itself faced with a
financial crisis, Italy did not possess reserves comparable with those of other countries. Her resources had
been impaired by the necessity of struggling against
the consequences of an overvalued lira. There had
already been big failures and expensive reconstructions in Italy before 1931. The Bank of Italy had
never been in a position to accumulate a gold reserve
comparable with that of France or even, relatively
speaking, with that of Holland, Switzerland, or Belgium.

What was the object of Signor Mussolini's decision to stabilise the lira at an overvalued level? Why did he disregard all warnings as to the consequences of his policy? Was he carried away by an unreasonable policy of prestige? Was it a sheer blunder due to inadequate realisation of the consequences of his act? Or did he have some motive in overvaluing the lira? This latter theory seems to be rather popular in some quarters where it is believed that in 1926 Signor Mussolini deliberately overvalued the lira in order to break the excessive power of financial and industrial interests. There can be no doubt that his action did break the influence of big industrialists and big bankers. Before the world crisis the depression had already compelled many leading industrial concerns and some important banks to fall back upon the Government in order to avoid the ruin brought by the overvaluation of the lira. From 1931 onwards this movement was intensified. Under the inexorable pressure of the depression, the leading banks had to relinquish their control over industrial and commercial undertakings which are now under the control of the Government. The power of the banks in Italy has been completely broken. While a few years ago Signor Toeplitz dared to defy Signor Mussolini, to-day the heads of the leading banks are to all intents and purposes Government officials in charge of the management of the commercial banking Department of the State. The big industrialists whose names are household words far beyond the frontiers of Italy are hardly more than paid managers in their own enterprises.

Whatever were Signor Mussolini's intentions in overvaluing the lira, the result was undoubtedly the

strengthening of his hands against the industrialists
and financiers. Was this result achieved deliberately
or did it just happen as things very often happen in
history? It is difficult to say. It is conceivable that
Signor Mussolini was anxious to reduce the influence
of bankers and industrialists. It is necessary to bear
in mind in judging his attitude and his actions that he
began his career as a Socialist and in more than one way
he has remained a Socialist. He had to make use of
the banking and industrial interests before the March
on Rome in order to be able to finance his movement.
Industrialists and financiers hoped to make use of
him as a means to fight Communism. Their assistance
was valuable during the initial stages of Fascism in
Italy. It was morally impossible for Signor Mussolini
to turn against those who had helped him immediately
after he assumed power in 1922. Possibly even politically it would have been difficult to defy the right wing
of his party by moving to the left. Is it reasonable
to assume that Signor Mussolini decided to free himself from the influence of those who had helped him
to power by the Machiavellian device of a deflationary
policy? In the author's opinion it is unthinkable that
he should have deliberately inflicted depression upon
the whole country merely in order to weaken the
power and influence of a certain group of people. By
1927 his position had been sufficiently consolidated
to be able to achieve the same end by direct and
straightforward methods. The fact that in face of
the unanimous opposition of banking and industrial
interests he decided to overvalue the lira shows that
he was completely master of the situation. There was
no need for him to apply underhand methods to
attain his end.

## (3) THE CORPORATE STATE

Another theory is that the deliberate overvaluation of the lira served the purpose of developing the Corporate State. It is beyond doubt that during periods of prosperity it is difficult to assail the strongholds of economic liberalism. The success of captains of industry in producing big profits, in expanding their undertakings, and in increasing production is presented as a triumph of individual initiative made possible by *laissez-faire*. It is only during periods of depression, and more especially during periods of acute crisis, that there is a tendency favouring Government intervention at the expense of *laissez-faire*. During such periods the prestige of the captains of industry and super-financiers inevitably declines. It becomes evident that in times of emergency they have to fall back upon the Government which controls the ultimate source of support. This tendency has been amply evident during the last few years. Under the pressure of crisis and depression practically all countries have departed to a large extent from economic liberalism. Apart altogether from countries such as Russia, Italy, and Germany, where the political system favours a high degree of State control, even in countries where Parliamentary democracy has remained unimpaired, Government intervention and planning has made considerable progress. In the United States it assumed under President Roosevelt the form of the New Deal. In Great Britain, Mr Elliot's marketing schemes have been the outstanding examples of a trend which is making progress in a less conspicuous way. In France, M. Laval has adopted measures for the defence of the franc which amount to an extremely high degree of interference with economic life and private contracts. By decree, house owners and certain types of undertakings have been ordered to reduce their charges by 10 per cent. At the same time, the interest rates fixed in private contracts have been reduced by decree to a corresponding extent. There is also a scheme in France for the cartelisation of industries which has all the characteristics of economic Fascism. In Belgium the Government has increased its power to control production and trade in order to cope with the extremely difficult situation caused by the overvaluation of the belga, and after its devaluation M. Van Zeeland embarked upon a thoroughgoing interventionist policy. Outside Europe, Canada is moving towards adopting the New Deal, while Japan has gone a long way towards economic Fascism.

On the basis of these facts it is possible to argue that the existence of conditions necessitating increased State intervention facilitated the development of the Corporate State in Italy, and that it is conceivable that in order to be able to help the Corporate system Signor Mussolini deliberately created conditions in which its adoption would meet with least resistance. This theory again, like the previous one, credits him with a degree of Machiavellism which in the author's view he does not possess. He certainly did not possess it in 1926. It is unthinkable that he should have deliberately caused a depression in order to advance the development of the Corporate State, the conception of which was in 1926 in any case extremely vague. Moreover, while it is true that in countries of Parliamentary democracy State intervention cannot make progress in the absence of abnormal economic difficulties, under a dictatorship resistance to State intervention can easily be dealt with even during periods of prosperity. It is probable that the Corporate system in Italy owes its progress to the depression created by the overvaluation of the lira, but there can be no doubt that the same result would have been achieved sooner or later in the absence of abnormal economic conditions.

It is easier to reject theories attributing to Signor Mussolini sinister motives in deliberately overvaluing the lira than to put forward an alternative acceptable explanation. In the author's opinion the policy he adopted in Pesaro and has pursued ever since is explained by his orthodox outlook on all monetary matters. It is strange that while his economic policy should be utterly unorthodox, he should remain entirely under the influence of ultra-orthodox monetary doctrines. Usually extreme deflationism and the idol-worshipping of international monetary stability goes with a belief in economic *laissez-faire*. For some inscrutable reason Signor Mussolini combines a highly heterodox economic policy with a highly orthodox monetary policy. To be able to explain this attitude would require a much more thorough knowledge of Signor Mussolini's mental evolution than the author possesses.

## (4) DEFENCE OF THE LIRA

If it is difficult to explain why Signor Mussolini decided to overvalue the lira in 1927, it is even more difficult to understand why, once the mistake was committed, he should have persisted in what has come to be termed "the policy of Pesaro". The sacrifices involved in the defence of the lira at its overvalued

level have kept on increasing. As we stated above, the
economic depression in Italy that preceded the international economic crisis reduced the country's resisting
capacity to deflation. In 1931 Italy entered the international deflation race heavily handicapped by the
deflation inflicted upon her since 1926 by the policy
of Pesaro.

Notwithstanding this, Signor Mussolini succeeded
until the end of 1934 in resisting the adverse pressure
on the lira. The prophets who after the suspension of
the gold standard in Great Britain predicted that Italy
would be among the first countries to follow her
example proved to be wrong. The defence of the lira
was carried on with great technical skill and with an
utter disregard of the sacrifices involved. To some
extent the suffering caused by deflation was mitigated
by the unorthodox methods with which deflation was
applied. Instead of seeking to reduce prices by the
orthodox method of credit restriction, all-round reductions were carried out on two occasions, in 1931 and in
1934, by Government decree. These decrees imposed
cuts on salaries, wages, rents, prices, etc. In resorting
to this method, it was possible to reduce the iniquities caused by deflationary credit restriction. On the
surface this may appear a more drastic method than
the lowering of prices by the forced liquidation of
bankrupt stocks. It is undoubtedly the less popular
way of deflating, since the responsibility for the cuts
can unmistakably be traced to the Government. But
Signor Mussolini is not in the habit of shirking responsibilities. Instead of leaving the adjustment to take place
in the haphazard way customary under the system of
*laissez-faire,* he took the bull by the horns and enforced
the less popular but more efficient and equitable

method. Since wages, prices, and the cost of living were adjusted downward simultaneously, the losses and inconveniences caused by the rigidity of various items and the discrepancies thus arising between them and the more elastic items were reduced.

Notwithstanding this, it was impossible to get away from the inevitable adverse effects of deflation upon trade. The fall in prices created new weak positions and led to the necessity for official support for banks and industries. Those who argue that this was in accordance with the aims of economic Fascism misunderstand the fundamental principles of the Corporate system. The essential difference between State Socialism and the Corporate State is that in the latter it is not the Government's aim to obtain control over industries by acquiring their ownership. Government control in the Corporate State assumes the form of directing and supplementing individual initiative through the organisation provided by the corporations. Signor Mussolini has always regarded the acquisition of majority share holdings in banks and industrial undertakings as a necessary evil, and it has been his declared policy to resell these holdings to private investors as soon as possible. Thus, the effects of deflation in this sphere were not at all in accordance with his aims.

There was another reason why the acquisition of financial control over banks and industries was detrimental from the point of view of the Government's policy. The financial resources that had to be mobilised for that purpose could have been employed much more profitably in financing public works. It is impossible to deny that, considering the limited financial resources at the Government's disposal, Signor Mussolini has worked miracles in this direction. Land reclaiming, electrification, building activity, excavations, etc., have made spectacular progress during the last few years. It is easy to imagine how much more could have been achieved had the milliards required to support banks and industries against the effects of deflation been used for public works. Indeed, during 1934 the original public-works programme had to be curtailed owing to budgetary considerations. A stage was reached at which Signor Mussolini was confronted with the dilemma of choosing between the speedy execution of his favourite public-works schemes and the defence of the lira through a reduction in budgetary expenditure. The increase of the budgetary deficit caused by further deflation necessitated further curtailments in the Government's programme of public works. Already the amount allocated for that purpose had had to be reduced in 1934 by about one-third. The public-works programme had been conceived with expert knowledge; its object was not merely to create additional employment in times of depression, but to make important additions of a largely productive character to the national wealth. Its drastic curtailment for budgetary considerations was therefore a loss from more than one point of view.

Furthermore, excessive deflation has put the newly created Corporate system to a too severe and not altogether fair test. While politically deflation tends to facilitate the development of the Corporate State, economically it is detrimental. That system is now being elaborated in full detail, and the world has been watching with keen interest the results it will produce. The Corporate system entails a high degree of interference with individual freedom, which can only be justi-

fied if it increases human welfare by solving the problem
of scientifically planned production and distribution.
Should deflation continue in Italy, the unique organisation will exhaust its possibilities in its struggle
against trade depression. The world judges by results,
and in terms of positive progress. If all that can be said
for the system will be that, thanks to it, the effect of
deflationary depression was not as disastrous as it
might have been, the opponents of the idea of the
Corporate State will be triumphant, and not without
reason.

There is another consideration. As a result of the
exchange difference in favour of the lira, there is a
danger that Italy will lose her emigrants. They are
on the way towards becoming the "lost legions" of
Italy, just as the tens of thousands of English people
who transferred their residence abroad to escape
ruinous income-tax after the war have become the
"lost legions" of Great Britain. Until recently, Italians
abroad remained attached, to a remarkable degree,
to their country of origin. While they were loyal to
their adopted country, their hearts remained with
Italy. They remitted every cent they saved; they took
every opportunity to pay visits to their native land;
and they looked forward to settling there again once
they could afford to retire.

As a result of the high exchange rate of the lira,
these links with the motherland have gradually tended
to weaken. The result has been not merely the actual
loss expressed in the falling figures of emigrants' re-
mittances. Should this state of affairs be prolonged
for some years, Italians abroad might become altogether *deraciné*; they might lose the habit of regarding
Italy as their permanent home; and the process of

their assimilation in their adopted countries would
then become accelerated. The loss for Italy would
be more than merely so many milliards of lire.

### (5) SIGNOR MUSSOLINI'S FIRM ATTITUDE

Signor Mussolini is well aware of this and of many
other arguments against the defence of the lira at its
present overvalued parity. On the occasion of his inter-
view with the Duce in November 1934, the author
was astonished to see how well acquainted he was with
the case against deflation, notwithstanding the fact
that he was entirely surrounded by ultra-orthodox
advisers. He realised what he stood to lose by continuing the policy of Pesaro. He was aware of the unfair
losses inflicted by that policy upon large classes of
debtors in agriculture and other spheres, and yet, confronted with the dilemma of choosing between these
disadvantages and the abandonment of the Pesaro
policy, he has decided again and again in favour of the
latter. In December last, when the sharp decline in
the gold reserve brought the problem once more to
the forefront, he decided in favour of continuing to
defend the lira at its present parity. To that end he
prepared to use up the privately owned foreign assets
of Italian citizens, which would otherwise have constituted a valuable secondary reserve in case of emergency. Signor Mussolini is well aware of the importance
of possessing a substantial external reserve for the
requirements of national defence in case of a war, and
yet he was prepared to use up a large portion of this
reserve in order to bolster up the lira at its present
uneconomic level. In February last he decided to
impose restrictions upon the import of raw materials

which were essential for Italy in time of peace and
indispensable in time of war. What is more, in July
last he decided to allow the gold reserve ratio to
decline under the statutory minimum of 40 per cent.

What is the explanation of this stubborn determination to pursue a policy which is so evidently against
the interests of Italy and of Fascism? One thing is
certain. It is conceivable that in 1927 Signor Mussolini
decided to overvalue the lira because he did not
realise the grave consequences of this act, but this
explanation can be safely ruled out as far as the
maintenance of the lira at its present overvalued level
is concerned. It is possible that in 1927 the choice of the
rate of stabilisation was simply a leap in the dark. In
the meantime, however, Signor Mussolini has had
every opportunity to realise what it means to have to
struggle with an overvalued exchange. Apart altogether
from the lessons taught by the experience of the last
seven years, Signor Mussolini's knowledge of economics
and finance has increased considerably during that
period. Those who had an opportunity of discussing
questions of finance with the Duce in 1927 maintain that
his knowledge at that time was highly inadequate. To
a very large extent he was dependent upon his advisers
and upon his instinct. The author was, however, very
favourably impressed by Signor Mussolini's grasp of
economics and finance at the end of 1934. To him, the
Duce appeared to have a good knowledge of both
fundamental principles and technical detail. He was
fully aware of the internal and international implications of his monetary policy. His decision to maintain
the lira at its present parity was, therefore, made with
open eyes. He fully realised the consequences of his
policy. This time there could be no question of his

decision having been due to an accidental blunder.

The theory that Signor Mussolini's attitude was due to considerations of prestige cannot be disposed of so lightly. Indeed, the majority of those with whom the writer discussed the question in Italy maintained that for considerations of prestige Signor Mussolini could not afford to depart from his policy of Pesaro. To the writer this argument sounded utterly unconvincing. Signor Mussolini would not have been the first statesman to change his monetary policy under the pressure of developments. Nor would monetary policy be the first sphere in which he would change his attitude. What is the use of being a Dictator if he has to pay more attention to the repercussions of his decisions upon public opinion than any constitutional Prime Minister? The main advantage of dictatorship over a Parliamentary system is exactly that it enables the Executive to disregard public opinion and to take unpopular decisions if they are in accordance with the public interest.

Moreover, it is by no means certain that the reaction of the Italian public to a devaluation of the lira would be unfavourable. It will be remembered that in England until September 20, 1931, ninety-nine people out of a hundred would have regarded the suspension of the gold standard as a major disaster, yet these very same people, twenty-four hours later, were obviously relieved that the gold standard had at last been suspended. Once it became an accomplished fact, everyone tried to make the best of it. In Italy of all countries, where the Press is entirely under the Government's control, it would be easy to bring about a change in public opinion.

## (6) THE PESARO PROMISE

Since so much importance is attached to the promise made by Signor Mussolini at Pesaro, it is essential to make plain exactly what Signor Mussolini promised. He stated that he would defend the lira "with the last drop of his blood". But what was exactly the meaning of his promise? To defend the lira against a depreciation. There was not a word in the Pesaro statement which could possibly be interpreted as a promise to increase the value of the lira.

At the time of the Pesaro speech the sterling-lira rate was 158; following upon the speech speculative buying brought about a sharp recovery, and in the following year it was stabilised at 92·46. This appreciation of the lira was a free gift to holders. It happened, not in execution of the Pesaro pledge, but in addition to it. Holders have no moral claim to the surplus on the basis of the promise made to them. It may be argued that it is not the letter of the statement that matters in the case of a moral obligation, but its spirit. Let us try, therefore, to analyse the inner meaning of Signor Mussolini's promise. In promising to defend the lira to the utmost, did he have its theoretical gold content in mind? Most unlikely. Did he think of the sterling and dollar rate? Equally improbable.

From the viewpoint of the Italian people, the only thing he could possibly have been concerned with was the internal purchasing power of the lira. To ninety-nine out of a hundred Italians it is a matter of indifference what is the gold content of the lira or even what sterling is worth in terms of lire. They are concerned with the amount of goods and services they can obtain for their lire. And it was this internal

I

value which Signor Mussolini must have had in mind
when promising to defend the lira. This is the common-
sense interpretation of the Pesaro statement.

What, in fact, has happened to the internal value
of the lira since the promise was made? At the time of
the speech the index number of wholesale prices was
over 700; even the annual average for 1926 was well
over 600. For 1934 this index number was about 275.
The decline in the cost of living, though naturally not
so marked as that of wholesale prices, was roughly
30 per cent. Thus, here again, as in the case of the
exchange value of the lira, Signor Mussolini did much
more than he promised. By virtue of the letter as well
as the spirit of his promise, he would only have had to
maintain prices and the cost of living where they were
in August 1926. So long as prices and the cost of living
were not allowed to rise above their 1926 level, he
would have carried out his pledge without fail.

But a situation in which prices will rise to anywhere
near their 1926 level is most unlikely. If, for the sake
of argument, the lira were to be devalued to the extent
of 50 per cent, the rise in prices caused by this act
would only cover a fraction of the distance between
the present level and the Pesaro level. We have seen
in the case of the United States that a devaluation of
41 per cent has caused wholesale prices to rise only by
a little over 20 per cent, while the cost of living has
risen by 8 per cent only. And this in spite of the fact
that it was the declared policy of President Roosevelt
to raise prices. If Signor Mussolini were to adopt the
opposite policy of endeavouring to minimise the effect
of the devaluation upon prices, any rise should be
proportionately even more moderate than in the
United States.

This point had to be discussed at some length because it carries immense weight in Italy. The main reason why most people do not believe in devaluation has been their misinterpretation of the Pesaro statement. If the correct interpretation were to be adopted officially, public opinion and expert opinion would swing round at one stroke.

It is not as if the relative number and strength of those for or against devaluation could influence the final decision. In France and elsewhere the issue may be fought out in the Cabinet Council, in Parliament, in the Press, amid the electorate, or even in the street. In Italy it will be fought out in the mind of one man. The Duce does not allow himself to be influenced by the weight of sectional interests; he may be mistaken but his sincerity is beyond doubt.

### (7) WAGES AND SAVINGS

It is believed that the reason why Signor Mussolini strongly resents any suggestion of devaluation made by industrialists is that he suspects attempts at reducing the workmen's real wages through a currency depreciation. And, although it is not adequately realised abroad, he goes out of his way to safeguard the interests of the working classes. Having outlawed strikes as a means of self-defence, he considers it a wise policy to see that the workmen get as fair a deal as is possible in existing conditions. In reality, the only chance workmen have for an increase in their real wages is through a devaluation of the lira. Wholesale prices always rise to a larger extent than the cost of living. If the result of a devaluation of the lira should be a rise in wholesale prices by, say, 20 per cent, while the cost of living rose by, say, 8 per cent—a proportion which roughly corresponds to experience in other countries—manufacturers would be able to afford an increase of wages, not only in proportion to the rise in the cost of living (in which case real wages would remain unchanged) but to a higher proportion, causing a rise in real wages.

Another reason why, it is said, he is unwilling to decide in favour of devaluation is that it would inflict unjust losses upon holders of Government securities, deposits, etc. It ought to be borne in mind, however, that the majority of investors and depositors owned their holdings before the fall in prices took place, or, at any rate, long before commodity prices approached their present low level. They stand to gain in purchasing power even after a reasonable devaluation of the lira.

There is, in any case, the position of debtors to be considered. Are they not entitled to justice and equity to the same extent as creditors? For years past they paid the price of the surplus purchasing power obtained by their creditors. Would it be unjust if in future they were to recover a fraction of the surplus they paid, as a result of a decline in the real burden of their debts?

All these considerations· and many others were brought to the attention of the Duce towards the end of last year. In spite of them, he decided once more to continue the defence of the lira. To some extent, however, he yielded to pressure in that he allowed the lira gradually to depreciate to the extent of some 8 per cent compared with its gold parity. The depreciation was so slow that it was almost imperceptible. Nevertheless, a discount of 8 per cent is incompatible with the rules of the gold standard, so that while in practice

Italian monetary policy remained based on the determination to defend the lira, in theory, at any rate, the gold standard was actually abandoned. In addition, drastic exchange control measures were adopted which were in themselves sufficient to amount to a suspension of the gold standard. Italy also introduced a system that had been in operation in Germany since the middle of 1934, payment for imports being made only as and when the foreign exchange became available for the purpose. The inevitable delays this method has caused in the settlement of commercial liabilities have done much harm to the financial and commercial prestige of Italy. From a moral point of view, it was certainly not worth while to defend the lira at the cost of drifting into the "gold insolvency standard".

Simultaneously with the adoption of exchange restrictions and import restrictions, the Italian Government endeavoured to base the foreign trade of the country as far as possible on clearing and compensation agreements. It hoped that in doing so it would succeed in securing a sufficient market for Italian goods to cover the amounts required for indispensable imports. Although the rise in commodity prices that followed the import restrictions further reduced the competitive capacity of Italian exporters, it was hoped that it would be possible to maintain the balance of payments at a reasonable equilibrium. Since foreign countries were anxious to sell to Italy, they might be induced to buy from her even though her prices were not competitive.

In Germany, the adoption of this system failed to produce the result that was expected, owing to the abnormal discrepancy between inland prices and the world level. It became necessary for Dr. Schacht to impose a special levy upon industry to finance the losses on exports. There is no reason to believe that it would have been otherwise in Italy.

### (8) THE ABYSSINIAN CONFLICT

The experiment was not, however, allowed to take its course undisturbed in Italy. A new element was introduced into the situation by the Abyssinian conflict. The increase in the production of armaments and the transport of Italian troops to East Africa affected the trade balance unfavourably. The adverse factors inherent in the situation thus became accentuated. In addition to having to use up privately owned foreign assets in supporting the lira at an uneconomic level, these resources had to be drawn upon heavily to finance the East African enterprise. In the circumstances, it was not altogether surprising to find one day that the Italian Government had decided to suspend the legal minimum gold reserve ratio of 40 per cent. Evidently it was coming to the end of its foreign exchange resources and had to make legal provisions that would enable it to draw upon the gold reserve more extensively than before.

Notwithstanding the increased pressure, Signor Mussolini continued to defend the lira at a discount of about 8 per cent. Although it cost much to buy the fuel and raw materials required in connection with the East African enterprise, the resources of the Bank of Italy continued to be wasted to bolster up the lira. And yet it is obvious that in the interests of the financing of the Abyssinian campaign it would be, from an Italian point of view, of vital importance to allow the lira to find its level. After its devaluation, some if not all the Italian capital that has taken refuge abroad would be repatriated. Italian exports would once more be competitive, and the deficit on the trade balance could be reduced. In spite of this, there has been, up to the time of writing, no sign of any change in Italian monetary policy, which as before remains substantially based on the Pesaro statement.

It remains to be seen how long Italy will be able to resist the trend towards the depreciation of the lira. Should the Abyssinian conflict develop into active hostilities, it would inevitably lead to the depreciation of the lira within a very short time. The only choice then would be between allowing it to depreciate gradually and devaluing it immediately.

It is sometimes suggested that Signor Mussolini means to use the conflict with Abyssinia as an excuse to devalue the lira. According to another theory, the Abyssinian conflict has been engineered to divert Italian public opinion from the adverse effects of the deflationary monetary policy. In the author's opinion, both theories are far too Machiavellian. The Italian ambitions in East Africa have nothing to do with considerations of monetary policy, but solely with the inadequate supply of raw material in Italy.

It remains to be seen whether Signor Mussolini will continue to defend the lira until it is swept off its present level by the deterioration of its technical position, or whether he will take deliberate action before the country has exhausted its gold reserve. The latter alternative would be by far the wiser course. Admittedly, so long as technically it is possible to continue the defence of the lira, it is not easy for Signor Mussolini to make up his mind. Indeed, he is confronted with what is probably one of the gravest dilemmas during the whole period of his reign. Since, however, the lira will have to be devalued sooner or later, his prolonged resistance to the inevitable only results in futile sacrifices. A nation can bleed away economically and financially as well as physically, and Signor Mussolini may realise sooner or later that no monetary dogma is worth that price.

# PRESIDENT ROOSEVELT THROUGH EUROPEAN EYES

## (1) INTRODUCTORY

THE enviable quality of being able to see ourselves as others see us is a rare gift, and the number of those who are wise enough to appreciate its advantage is small. When European writers express views on President Roosevelt's policy, as often as not their well-meaning efforts elicit sarcastic comments in the United States about "outsiders who pretend to know more about our problem than we do ourselves". The author encountered such a response on one or two occasions. When in his book *The Future of Gold* he ventured to express an opinion on the course President Roosevelt's monetary policy was likely to take, he was politely rebuked by a critic in the *Wall Street Journal* for having rushed in where Americans themselves feared to tread.

Although the author has followed developments in the United States during the past two years as closely as was possible from across the Atlantic, he is aware that he is at a disadvantage compared with those who have been able to observe things on the spot. And yet in a way the fact that he has been watching events from a distance has placed him at an advantage over local observers. The latter have been admittedly in a better position to ascertain the facts in all their details by direct first-hand experience. On the other hand, they have been in a less favourable position than the distant observer to form detached opinions and to appreciate the broad implications of the problems raised. Indeed, it is not without reason that American bankers, economists, Government officials, and politicians sometimes pay visits to London and other European centres with the declared object of ascertaining what is happening in the United States. While they are at home they are too closely connected with events to be able to regard them without prejudice. Their political allegiances and material interests are bound to influence their opinion, even though frequently only subconsciously, on the various measures taken by the Administration.

Admittedly, if it is difficult to find anybody in the United States whose views on President Roosevelt's policy are entirely free from prejudice, it is not much easier to find impartial observers of American events in Europe. After all, the effect of President Roosevelt's policy is not confined within the borders of the United States. His actions have a world-wide influence and bear upon the material welfare of everybody from China to Peru. The only claim to relative impartiality foreign observers can put forward is that they are not influenced by the political passions which blur the vision of American observers. Apart from this, there is every likelihood that the British expert will regard President Roosevelt's policy primarily from a British point of view, the French expert from the point of view of its effect upon France, and so forth.

To be forewarned is to be forearmed, and the author, being conscious of the influence of the British point of view on his opinions, has done his utmost to resist any tendency towards one-sidedness and to arrive at as impartial an opinion as is humanly possible. It is for readers to judge whether he has succeeded in this task. He must confess that his first reactions to the various measures introduced by the present Administration were inevitably influenced by their effect upon British interests. It was only subsequently, on second thoughts, that he succeeded in detaching himself sufficiently to regard developments from an American and from a generally international point of view. On many occasions he had to reconsider opinions he had formed at first.

## (2) SUSPENSION OF THE GOLD STANDARD

An act on which, on second thoughts, the author felt compelled to change his opinion completely was the suspension of the gold standard in the United States. At first he fully shared the indignation of the British Press and public opinion that followed this act in April 1933. He emphatically endorsed the opinion of those who maintained that there was no necessity whatsoever for President Roosevelt to suspend the gold standard. It is true that there was heavy and persistent pressure on the dollar, and that internal economic and financial conditions in the United States were chaotic. Nevertheless, the technical position of the dollar was strong, and the possession of huge gold reserves and a by no means unfavourable balance of payments would have enabled the American authorities to resist the selling pressure for a long time notwithstanding internal difficulties. The writer recalled the bitter criticism directed against Great Britain from the American side in 1931 for having suspended the gold standard, even though the British Government resorted to that act only after having exhausted completely its gold reserve by using up an equivalent

amount of Franco-American credits. There was no
sign of such a fight against the adverse pressure on
the dollar. While Great Britain was swept off the gold
standard, the United States "walked off" it.

Indeed, in his first indignation, the author, in
common with many others in England and on the
Continent, failed to discover any mitigating circum-
stance to justify or excuse President Roosevelt's
action. In common with many British experts he
believed that the depreciation of the dollar was a
move directed primarily against Great Britain, and
that its main object was to enable Americans to
undersell British exporters. While he had no objection
to Great Britain's enjoying the advantages of a depreciated exchange at the expense of the United
States between September 1931 and April 1933, he
strongly resented the attempt of the United States
to enjoy similar advantages at the expense of Great
Britain—an example of how opinions are subconsciously influenced by material interests.

Doubtless the suspension of the gold standard in
the United States was an unexpected blow to British
interests. Apart altogether from its direct effect upon
foreign trade, it deprived Great Britain of a highly
valuable bargaining counter. It had been hoped in
London that we might be able to obtain considerable
advantages in the form of war debt cancellation and
commercial treaties in return for the stabilisation of
sterling. Before the suspension of the gold standard in
the United States, it had seemed that Great Britain
would be in a position practically to dictate terms at
an international conference owing to the keenness of
the United States and other countries for an early
stabilisation agreement.

Before April 1933, Great Britain evidently held all the trumps in the supreme game of international finance. It was overlooked in London that too strong a hand might prove a disadvantage. There is an old-fashioned game of cards called "ombre" in which a player who holds all the trumps can be defeated by his opponent who holds none. His declaration of *grandissimo* may be followed by a declaration of *nullissimo* on the part of his opponent, who wins the game by the weakness of his hand. This possibility ought to have occurred to British interests in 1933, since they themselves had benefited from it in 1931, when they answered the triumphant *grandissimo* of France with an unassuming but none the less effective *nullissimo*. In 1931 France held all the trumps and Great Britain none. Yet Great Britain won the game by going off the gold standard. Her weakness became her strength. History repeated itself in 1933, but this time it was Great Britain who held the trumps, thanks to the depreciation of sterling, and it was the United States who unexpectedly declared *nullissimo* by going off the gold standard. Had the British Government realised early in 1933 that this might happen, it would presumably have been prepared to do its utmost to prevent it; in all probability it would even have been prepared to stabilise rather than expose itself to the possibility of a competitive depreciation of the dollar. But in London everybody was convinced that so long as the American monetary authorities possessed a huge gold reserve there was no danger of a suspension of the gold standard. To go off gold without being driven off it appeared inconceivable.

## (3) AN INEVITABLE STEP

It was thus not surprising that when President Roosevelt did this inconceivable thing the first response in Great Britain should have been an outburst of indignation. Admittedly, to a very large extent this indignation was the result of annoyance at the calling of our bluff. To some extent, however, it was due to the fact that people on this side did not realise how desperate internal conditions in the United States were at the beginning of 1933. The author himself did not at the time consider that internal American conditions were sufficiently bad to justify President Roosevelt's action. It was only subsequently, on closer examination of the circumstances, that he arrived at the conclusion that the suspension of the gold standard was inevitable, even though he was aware that it would have been possible to have postponed it for a while. But even if the truth of this had been adequately realised, it is doubtful whether it would have made any difference to the British attitude towards President Roosevelt's action. In 1933 it was still considered that it was the supreme duty of every country to defend the gold standard until it had completely exhausted its resources. Even if a Government realised that there was no hope of saving the currency, it was held to be its moral duty to hold out until the depletion of its gold stocks made further resistance technically impossible. It was strongly resented that President Roosevelt had not been prepared to go in for such heroics, and that, instead of playing Sir Galahad at the expense of his nation, he preferred to yield to the inevitable before and not after the gold resources of his country were exhausted.

In the author's opinion it is to the credit of President Roosevelt that he realised how utterly hopeless it was to try to defend the dollar at its old parity, and that he was not prepared to sacrifice the country's gold reserves for the sake of mistaken considerations of prestige and of false pride. It must have been evident to him that in the long run internal conditions in the United States were bound in any case to lead to the collapse of the dollar. Had the banks which got into difficulties in February 1933 been allowed to fail, the panic thus created would have driven milliards of American capital abroad, and this would have exhausted the gold stock of the Federal Reserve Banks. Had it been decided to grant wholesale support to the banks, this again would have brought about inflation on such a scale as to make it impossible to maintain the dollar at its gold parity. The only possible way of allaying the panic was by arousing hopes of recovery, and the depreciation of the dollar was the only possible means to that end. Excessive private indebtedness was at the root of the trouble. As a result of the heavy fall in commodity prices, the burden of this indebtedness became unbearable and innumerable debtors found themselves hopelessly insolvent. The American public was well aware that the banks were involved in these insolvencies to the extent of many milliards. It would have been impossible to restore the confidence of depositors towards banks otherwise than by arousing hopes of a rise in commodity prices which would restore the solvency of debtors and of banks. Had this not been done by suspending the gold standard, it would have been necessary to double the public debt and to inflate the currency to a fantastic degree in order to enable the banks to meet the withdrawals of deposits.

The result would have been a persistent selling pressure on the dollar which in the long run would have exhausted the gold stock of the United States.

Evidently the dollar was doomed. President Roosevelt, on assuming office, was faced with the alternative, not of suspending or maintaining the gold standard, but of suspending it immediately while still in possession of large gold reserves or of postponing its suspension for six or twelve months while using up the gold reserves. Is he to blame for having been practical rather than melodramatic? It would have served no useful purpose to have prolonged the agony, though it would have satisfied the moralists. It was the predecessors of these romantic moralists who had great admiration for General Lopez, the ruthless dictator of Paraguay in the nineteenth century, who by the sheer force of his personality compelled his nation to bleed to death rather than surrender and give up a hopeless fight. A nation can bleed away financially as well as physically, and it is to the credit of President Roosevelt that he did not choose this futile course.

## (4) A BLESSING IN DISGUISE

His action is subject to much criticism on the ground that it has created a dangerous precedent. His critics maintain that it was the first time the gold standard had been abandoned by a leading country as a matter of expediency. The untenability of these criticisms is obvious to those who, like the author, have come to realise that the suspension of the gold standard in the United States was in any case only a question of time.

Apart altogether from this, it may well be asked whether it would not be to the best interest of mankind if the suspension of the gold standard should come to be regarded as a matter of expediency. After all, the international stability of a currency is only a means to an end and not an end in itself. It should be maintained so long as the sacrifices involved do not outweigh the advantages it yields. One of the main reasons for the suffering of the world during the past five years has been the conception that the international stability of currencies has to be maintained in any circumstances irrespective of the cost involved. The maintenance of a currency at its gold parity has come to be regarded as a religious dogma which cannot be questioned. If President Roosevelt had done nothing more than prove to the world that it was possible to disregard this dogma, he would have earned the gratitude of mankind.

Even if his decision is regarded from a purely British point of view, the author cannot help feeling that it was a blessing in disguise. Admittedly, it was very much in disguise. Few people were able to see it at the time. The author himself was at first convinced that the suspension of the gold standard in the United States was the heaviest blow that had fallen on Great Britain since the Central European financial crisis of 1931. Doubtless, taking a short view, British interests had no reason to be pleased. The depreciation of the dollar soon made itself felt in international markets and British exporters had to cope with the increased competitive power of their American rivals. Apart from this, from April 1933, Great Britain had to relinquish her supremacy in the sphere of international finance, which it had held ever since September 1931. The world's eyes were no longer directed on London but on Washington. Having become used to leading, London

K

was none too pleased at having to play second fiddle. The British authorities realised to their dismay that they were no longer undisputed masters of British monetary policy, which to a large extent had to be adjusted to take into account American policy. At that time this appeared to most people a grave disadvantage. Many of us have since come to realise that it was in reality an advantage, for British monetary policy had been much too timid and was in strong need of the influence of the bolder policy pursued by President Roosevelt. What would have happened if the United States had remained on a gold basis? In all probability sterling would have been stabilised by now, presumably in the vicinity of something like 86 francs to the pound, at which level it was maintained for a long time during the summer of 1933. There would have been no rise in commodity prices in Great Britain or abroad, and the deflationary influence of the overvaluation of the dollar, the franc, and other gold currencies would have continued to depress world prices.

The author is convinced that in order to make the huge burden of British public debt bearable a drastic devaluation of sterling is an absolute necessity. Even if this were realised in official quarters in Great Britain, it would nevertheless be unthinkable that the British authorities should so break with their orthodox traditions as to cause sterling deliberately to depreciate. Their hand was forced, however, by President Roosevelt's policy. If, when sterling is stabilised, the level chosen is not unduly high, Great Britain will have to thank President Roosevelt for it.

## (5) THE LONDON ECONOMIC CONFERENCE

The truth of this is realised to-day by many of those who were outraged by the rapid depreciation of the dollar before and during the London Economic Conference in June and July 1933. During those days the fall of the dollar was watched with helpless rage in London, not only by the representatives of the gold countries but also by British interests, even though the latter had the remedy in their own hands in the form of a corresponding depreciation of sterling against gold. President Roosevelt was easily the best-hated man in the world during those memorable days in the Geological Museum of South Kensington. Nor did his popularity increase after his famous message of July 3, 1933, in which he made it plain in somewhat undiplomatic terms that there could be no question of stabilising the dollar until it had reached a level which he considered adequately low. This bombshell shattered the dream of those who had hoped that their subtle devices to induce the United States to stabilise the dollar would prove successful.

It will be remembered that, during the early days of the Economic Conference, negotiations were carried on between representatives of the American, British, and French Treasuries and banks of issue to arrive at a plan by which exchange fluctuations could be avoided during the Economic Conference. There was, in fact, some kind of "gentlemen's agreement" concluded, by which it was agreed that without any formal undertaking to that effect the British and American authorities would endeavour to keep their exchanges as stable as possible. It was hoped by those favouring the immediate stabilisation of sterling and dollar at a high

level that if the exchanges were kept *de facto* stable
for a sufficient length of time, it would be easier to
work up public opinion in Great Britain and the United
States in favour of a *de jure* stabilisation on the basis of
the existing rates. To those who entertained such hopes
President Roosevelt's outspoken message came like a
bolt from the blue. The representatives of the continental gold countries were speechless with indignation. Even amongst the British experts there were but
few who realised that, far from fighting against Great
Britain, President Roosevelt was in fact fighting for
Great Britain's interests at the same time as for those
of the United States.

Admittedly, the tone of the message was unneces-
sarily offensive. The author saw M. Rist, one of the
chief French delegates to the Economic Conference,
talking to a group of journalists in the lobby, and
referring to Mr Roosevelt's remark on "old-fashioned
fetishes" almost with tears in his eyes. The harshness
of President Roosevelt's tone was subject to criticism
even in quarters which otherwise approved of his
policy. But it was perhaps necessary for him to speak
to Europe in that tone in order to strengthen his
position at home. Indeed, as far as it was possible to
judge from this side, the very outspoken manner in
which he dealt with the London gathering disarmed
much of his domestic opposition. The author had some
personal experience which confirmed this impression.
During the Economic Conference two Republican
politicians, Senator Moses and Colonel Knox of the
*Chicago Daily News*, were in London with watching
briefs. Neither of them had any reason to be particularly partial to President Roosevelt; indeed, their
object was to collect evidence which might be used

against him. Notwithstanding this, they were both overjoyed when the message of July 3 arrived. "I would not have thought it possible", one of them told the author, "that I should ever drink the health of Roosevelt." If two highly intelligent politicians of the opposition were thus converted, for the moment, in favour of the President, it is easy to imagine the degree to which he increased his popularity among the general public at home by lecturing Europe in the tone he did. Those who realise how important it was for him for the success of his policy to obtain widespread support can hardly blame him for addressing the London Conference in a style that was meant for home consumption. In any case, the London gathering deserved what it got, and more.

The representatives of the Gold Bloc felt, however, outraged, and decided to retaliate by wrecking the Conference. The next few weeks were spent in a struggle between those who wanted to close the Conference forthwith and those who were desirous of preserving appearances and carrying on for a while. In the end the Conference dragged on until the end of July without producing any result. Needless to say, President Roosevelt was blamed by the European Press for its failure. It was said that, so long as it was not known at what level the dollar would be stabilised, the Conference could serve no useful purpose and that President Roosevelt, in refusing to stabilise the dollar, had prevented it from producing any constructive results. In the author's opinion, however, President Roosevelt can hardly be blamed for refusing to subordinate his plans to the success of the Economic Conference. But he is open to criticism for having agreed to the Conference at all so long as he was not

prepared to stabilise, and so long as he did not even
know how far it would be necessary for him to depreciate the dollar. Given the fact of the uncertainty
of the American monetary policy, the Conference was
unquestionably foredoomed. With a little foresight and
tact, President Roosevelt might have spared the world
this disappointment. Apart from the unnecessary ex-
citement and irritation caused by the London Conference, its failure ruled out the possibility of another
Conference for a long time, and discredited in advance
any attempt to arrange one even if conditions were to
become more favourable. The only possible explanation is that President Roosevelt did not know his own
mind. The indecision which characterised his attitude
was largely responsible for minimising the favourable
effect of his policy.

It appeared at one time during the Economic Conference as if the aggressively uncompromising attitude
of President Roosevelt might drive Great Britain into
the arms of the newly formed Gold Bloc. That this did
not happen was largely due to two causes: the revolt
of the Dominions—said to have been engineered by
Sir Henry Strakosch—against linking up their currencies with gold while the dollar was depreciating,
and the destructive attitude taken up by the gold
countries in endeavouring to wreck the Conference.
Thanks to these influences the British Government
decided to adopt a neutral attitude half-way between
that of President Roosevelt and the Gold Bloc. The
events of the next six months proved that in the long
run British monetary policy was inclined to follow
President Roosevelt rather than to strengthen its links
with the countries on gold.

## (6) THE GOLD-BUYING POLICY

The next shock Europe received from Washington was the announcement of President Roosevelt's gold-buying policy in October 1933. Until then there was no actual evidence of any deliberate and direct action on the part of the American authorities to depreciate the dollar. From October 25, 1933, however, it became the declared policy of President Roosevelt to cause the dollar to depreciate by raising the official buying price of gold. The announcement of this policy caused deep anxiety in Europe, and there was no lack of hostile comment in Great Britain and on the Continent. President Roosevelt was accused of pursuing a destructive policy, calculated to inflict heavy losses upon Europe, to endanger the moderate progress made by Great Britain since 1931, and to drive several countries off the gold standard.

Admittedly, his gold policy was a crude and brutal method of attaining the desired end. In addition to the direct losses inflicted upon Europe, it also created an atmosphere of uncertainty, since nobody knew how far President Roosevelt intended to go. It is true that Congress limited his authority to depreciate the dollar to 50 cents, but most people in Europe took it for granted that there would be no difficulty in lowering the legal limit. The first reaction to President Roosevelt's announcement of his new policy was scepticism as to the possibilities of his scheme being successful. The experts on this side of the Atlantic pointed out that since there was no free gold arbitrage between the United States and Europe, the gold price fixed by President Roosevelt above the world parity was bound to be ineffective. When in the course of November

1933 the dollar was inclined to lag far behind the movement of its gold parity, these critics triumphantly pointed out that the scheme had failed. A little later, however, the depreciation of the dollar caught up the downward movement of its gold parity and went in fact temporarily even beyond it. There were some bad-tempered comments in consequence, and it was not until President Roosevelt temporarily stabilised the dollar on January 30, 1934, that the atmosphere of hostility subsided.

The author must confess again that he was amongst those who strongly disapproved of President Roosevelt's gold policy. As in the case of the decision to suspend the gold standard, his first reaction was one of indignation at the deliberate act of currency depreciation and its ruthless method. Yet, he had later to admit that after all President Roosevelt was right. The President realised that there was little chance of raising commodity prices without a drastic devaluation of the dollar. His efforts to reflate would have failed to produce even a limited result had they not been backed up and consolidated by devaluation.

From a purely American point of view, President Roosevelt was undoubtedly right. From a British point of view, the effect of his action depended entirely on the British attitude towards it. Had the British authorities refused to allow sterling to follow the dollar—in fact at one time they allowed the sterling-dollar rate to rise to 5·50—they would have had to bear the burden of President Roosevelt's policy in company with the countries of the Gold Bloc. As, however, sterling was allowed to adjust itself gradually to the dollar, there is no reason to believe that the damage to British interests was heavy. If British ex-

port trade did suffer, it was because sterling was not allowed during 1934 to adjust itself completely to its new economic parity with the dollar. Most of the time it was around 5 dollars, and towards the end of the year it declined to the vicinity of its old mint parity, but it remained nevertheless considerably above its economic parity, which is estimated to be rather under 4·50. Had the British Exchange Equalisation Account not supported sterling to an excessive degree during the greater part of 1934, it would undoubtedly have declined to that level.

In that case President Roosevelt might have resumed his deliberate depreciation of the dollar by raising the official buying price of gold, and the depreciation of sterling below its old parities would have led to the much-dreaded "currency depreciation race" between the two countries. It is a matter of opinion whether such a development would necessarily have been an evil or whether the two countries, in trying to outbid each other in currency depreciation, would in fact have done the right thing in the wrong way and for the wrong reason. Since the author is convinced that nothing but a drastic devaluation of all leading currencies can provide a satisfactory final solution, he is inclined to hold the latter view. He does not believe that President Roosevelt's gold-buying policy was in any way harmful to British interests. On the contrary, it prevented the British authorities from stabilising sterling at too high a level, and from this point of view the author regrets that President Roosevelt has not until now gone much further.

Needless to say, the countries of the Gold Bloc have had to suffer through the depreciation of the dollar and of the currencies of the Sterling Bloc. They have,

however, only themselves to blame for having pursued a stubborn policy of deflation instead of adopting a realistic attitude by devaluing their currencies or allowing them to find their level in the changed circumstances. But even from the narrow point of view of the defence of the existing parities of gold currencies, President Roosevelt's gold policy was at the time of its application a blessing in disguise. It will be remembered that the deliberate depreciation of the dollar at the end of 1933 and the beginning of 1934 coincided with one of the periodical climaxes in the French financial and political crisis. That the troubles early in 1934 did not lead to a flight from the franc on a much larger scale than they actually did was due to the fact that the deliberate depreciation of the dollar and the likelihood of sterling following it diverted attention from the vulnerable position of the franc. It was difficult for Frenchmen to decide where to export their capital, considering that both sterling and the dollar were likely to depreciate further. To some extent, the flight from the franc assumed the form of gold hoarding, but it would have assumed to a much larger extent the form of transfers to London and New York had it not been for the deliberate depreciation of the dollar, which diverted attention from the inherent weakness of the franc. Thus, it may be said that, far from tending to wreck the gold currencies, President Roosevelt had in fact saved them during one of their critical periods. Needless to say, if we take a long view it is evident that the depreciation of sterling and the dollar have considerably aggravated the difficulties of France and other countries of the Gold Bloc, but the fact remains that at the time when President Roosevelt was accused of trying to wreck the franc, he was in reality aiding it. What is more, the author is convinced that if in the long run President Roosevelt's policy were to result in the devaluation of the remaining gold currencies, it would be to the good of all parties concerned. International equilibrium can only be restored through the devaluation of all currencies, which at the same time should go a long way towards reducing the burden of excessive national and international indebtedness.

## (7) POLICY OF REFLATION

Hitherto we have only been dealing with the repercussions upon Europe of President Roosevelt's monetary policy in the international sphere. The next step is to explain the European point of view regarding his internal monetary policy. The author is among the few Europeans who realise that the object of President Roosevelt's monetary policy during 1933 and 1934 was first and foremost internal and not international. While in the case of Great Britain the improvement of the trade balance through a depreciation of sterling was a question of primary importance, in the case of the United States considerations of foreign trade were quite secondary. If President Roosevelt wanted to depreciate the dollar, it was not in order to increase American exports—although its results in the sphere of foreign trade were by no means unwelcome—but in order to reduce the burden of excessive domestic private indebtedness and to cause a revival of home trade. That this was his object was indicated by the various measures taken to stimulate the rise in commodity prices in the home market. Had President Roosevelt intended to concentrate upon increasing exports, he would have followed the British example

by endeavouring to prevent the depreciation of the
dollar from producing its effect upon internal prices.
This is what actually happened in Great Britain when,
simultaneously with the suspension of the gold standard, the British Government resorted to drastic deflationary measures such as the increase of the bank rate,
all-round economies, and crushing taxation. Far from
embarking upon such a policy, President Roosevelt
spared no efforts to reflate internally. Indeed, even his
deliberate action of depreciating the international
value of the dollar merely served the purpose of
internal inflation. The milliards he spent on relief and
public works and his endeavours to compel employers
to raise wages leave no doubt in this respect. Such
evidence of his intention to raise commodity prices
should have been sufficient to allay suspicions in Great
Britain that President Roosevelt's policy was directed
against British export trade.

Doubtless the necessity of raising commodity prices
was realised also in Great Britain, and although the
first panic measures taken in 1931 effectively prevented
the rise which would otherwise have taken place, in
subsequent years the Government declared itself in
favour of a higher price-level. That, however, was about
all that it was prepared to do to attain that end apart
from some mild measures favouring cheap money.
Indeed, the attitude of the British Government towards raising prices was somewhat similar to the attitude of a well-known hero of Oscar Wilde who said
that he was prepared to do anything to keep young
except get up early, take exercise, and lead a moderate
life. The British Government too was prepared to do
anything to raise commodity prices except take any
action to attain that end. In the circumstances it owes

a debt of gratitude to President Roosevelt, who has
done all the work facilitating a moderate rise in British
commodity prices, which would not have taken place
but for his reflationary measures. These measures were
applied internally, but inevitably produced an international effect and, to some extent the British price-
level has also benefited by them. The benefits derived
from the American reflation by the raw-material-producing British Dominions and colonies were, needless
to say, much more evident than those enjoyed by the
motherland. As, however, the prosperity of the latter
largely depends upon the welfare of the Empire, the
indirect advantages obtained by Great Britain through
President Roosevelt's reflationary policy have been
considerable. While opinion in Great Britain is divided
as to President Roosevelt's policy of depreciating the
dollar, there can be no two opinions in Great Britain
or in Europe as to his price-raising efforts. It has
obviously been to the interest of Great Britain and of
Europe that his endeavours should be successful. If
President Roosevelt should succeed in raising commodity prices even further, it would be highly beneficial to Europe, quite irrespective of any movement of
European prices. If price-levels in Europe follow commodity prices in the United States, the rising trend
would improve economic and financial conditions on
this side of the Atlantic, while at the same time lowering the burden of indebtedness. If European prices lag
behind American prices, European foreign trade should
benefit as a result of the decline of the competitive
capacity of American trade. Thus, Europe could only
gain by President Roosevelt's success in raising commodity prices in the United States. Notwithstanding
this, he has been subject to sharp criticism in Europe

on account of his price-raising policy. He has been attacked not only by orthodox economists but also by statesmen holding responsible positions on the Continent. They have failed to realise that prosperity in their countries would have been furthered to no slight degree if the much-criticised Roosevelt experiment were to succeed. It almost appears as though orthodox economists and statesmen would much rather have seen the world doomed by strictly orthodox methods than saved by the unorthodox methods applied by President Roosevelt. They were afraid of his success because it would have thrown their own failure into stronger relief. For this reason, they spared no effort to minimise the significance of any progress reported from the United States and to accentuate any setback or disadvantages that accompanied President Roosevelt's efforts. In their gloomier moods they predicted collapse and chaos in the United States, and in their brighter moods they indulged in sneers and sarcasm.

It was not until about the end of 1934 that continental statesmen realised that in reality President Roosevelt was fighting their battle. Having realised that they could deflate no further, they decided to rely upon his reflationary policy to obviate the necessity for them to deflate or devalue. The tone of official statements concerning President Roosevelt's policy changed completely and the French Finance Minister, M. Germain-Martin, went so far as to wish him the best of luck.

## (8) THE SILVER-BUYING POLICY

The next shock administered by President Roosevelt to Europe and the rest of the world was the announcement of his silver-buying policy in 1934. It was greeted with triumphant joy in the camp of bimetallists, which has grown in strength considerably since 1931. Bimetallism in England has found supporters among influential business men, politicians, economists, etc., but has failed to produce the least influence on the official monetary policy. Their dwindling hopes were raised considerably by President Roosevelt's announcement of his intention to include silver in the note cover, to raise its price, and to purchase large amounts. Outside the select but small camp of bimetallists, there was little cause for enthusiasm. Possibly in official quarters the opportunity for unloading Indian silver at favourable prices was welcomed, but business circles interested in trade with China were worried about the probable consequences of President Roosevelt's silver policy upon that country. Subsequent developments in China proved that their pessimism was only too well founded.

In the author's opinion there is a great deal to be said in favour of including silver, to a limited extent and on the basis of its market value, in the note cover, in order to broaden the metallic basis for possible credit expansion. On the other hand, raising the price of silver to the figure President Roosevelt has in mind is an experiment which may cut both ways, and the chances are that its disadvantages will more than outweigh its advantages. Besides the maintenance of the price at its high level would present insurmountable difficulties. The average British view is not nearly as much against the partial remonetisation of silver as would appear from the Press, which in this respect is not adequately representative of the country's opinion. On the other hand, in continental countries, the idea of remonetisation, however limited, is emphatically rejected, and President Roosevelt's decision to include silver in the note cover is regarded as a first-rate obstacle to the re-establishment of a uniform international monetary standard.

## (9) THE NEW DEAL

While Europe is too closely concerned with President Roosevelt's monetary policy to view it without prejudice, it is much easier to find detached observers of his general economic policy outside the monetary sphere. Needless to say, opinions are sharply divided about his New Deal. Ultra-Conservative quarters were shocked by the fact that a statesman who was evidently not a Socialist should inaugurate a policy aimed at raising wages. In Europe the attitude of non-Socialist Governments has always been in favour of maintaining wages at a low level, so as to increase the competitive capacity of the countries' trade. Indeed, in the continental gold countries the reduction of wages has been raised to the level of a first-class civic virtue. Orthodox economists, always ready to provide a theoretical basis for practical reactionary thought, declared the inelasticity of wages to be the main source of all our difficulties. When talking about inelasticity, they of course referred to the reluctance of workmen to agree to wage cuts during a period of falling prices and depressed trade. They had nothing to say about the reluctance of employers to raise wages during a period of rising prices and prosperous trade. Elasticity of wages in the upward direction is in fact considered in the orthodox camp as undesirable from the point of view of progress and prosperity. The view is held that it is only if wages do not rise in proportion to increasing profits that the amounts required for capital expenditure can be made available on a sufficiently large scale out of current earnings. Those who hold such views do not take into consideration the adverse effect of the maldistribution of purchasing power. Even the experience of the last boom, which assumed exaggerated dimensions and was fated to collapse exactly because it led to profit inflation and to an inadequate distribution of increased earnings, failed to teach them a lesson.

In the circumstances, it is not surprising that President Roosevelt's New Deal policy should come as a shock to many quarters in Europe. The idea that a bourgeois Government should commit itself to a policy favouring higher wages in the interest of trade recovery met with strong disapproval, especially on the Continent. In England the orgy of wage cuts passed its climax in 1931, and there has been a growing movement in non-Socialistic quarters favouring the restoration of cuts. For this reason, President Roosevelt's policy has met with a certain degree of understanding. On the Continent, however, as far as the countries of the Gold Bloc are concerned, lower wages and still lower wages have continued to remain the password. The example provided by President Roosevelt was for this reason anything but welcome. Conceivably it increased in some instances the resistance of workmen's unions against deflationary cuts, and thus added to the difficulties of the Governments in bringing about the much-desired readjustments in a downward direction.

But even in quarters where the principle involved in President Roosevelt's New Deal policy was favoured, there was much criticism of details. It was felt that

L

in this respect, as in many other respects, President Roosevelt was doing the right thing in the wrong way. The view was held that to raise wages before prices had actually risen and trade improved was putting the cart before the horse, and that it might easily nip in the bud any trade recovery that would otherwise have taken place. There were many other misgivings as to details in quarters friendly towards the principle of the New Deal, but on the whole it was felt in progressive quarters that the recognition of the principle itself was a great thing, and that it would produce a profound influence all over the world.

The high degree of interference with economic activity practised by the National Recovery Administration and other administrative organisations has, needless to say, been subject to criticism in quarters which represent the last strongholds of *laissez-faire* in Europe. The majority of academic economists in England, and to an even larger extent in the countries of the Gold Bloc, are strongly against President Roosevelt, not merely because of his anti-deflationary policy but at least to the same degree because of his policy of Government intervention. These diehards of economic liberalism strongly resent the fact that a Government which is neither Communist nor Fascist should interfere with the freedom of business life to such a high degree. They are afraid that should President Roosevelt's experiment prove successful it will strengthen the movement against *laissez-faire* in their own countries. In any case, economic planning and Government intervention are making headway in every part of Europe, largely under the influence of the initiative taken by President Roosevelt. *Laissez-faire* economists have been hoping, however, that this move-

public debt. Admittedly, a country with the gigantic resources of the United States can well afford to increase its public debt, especially as its total is still considerably below the figure of the British public debt, though the national wealth of Great Britain bears no comparison with that of the United States. At the same time, it is impossible to view the rapid increase of the deadweight debt without a certain amount of misgiving. Unless there is a substantial increase in commodity prices to offset the additional burden, it is to be feared that the balance-sheet of the public-works policy may close with a heavy debit balance. Much depends, of course, upon the nature and value of real wealth created as a consequence of the increase in the public debt. If the result should be an increase in the productive capacity of the United States and a general increase in wealth and welfare, the country will be in a better position to stand the burden of increased public debt than it is at present to bear the burden of its relatively moderate Government indebtedness.

However it may be, it is certain that in this sphere President Roosevelt's policy has influenced to no slight degree the attitude of many European Governments. There is, in fact, reason to believe that even the British Government, which has hitherto rigidly refused to embark upon a policy of public works will have to yield to this influence in the course of the next year or two. Public opinion in Great Britain has been profoundly impressed by the possibilities of improving the standard of living and reducing unemployment by the aid of public works. Demand for a really ambitious scheme of slum clearance is becoming stronger and stronger and the Government can hardly afford to remain out of touch with public opinion. In other European countries, too, President Roosevelt's example is forcing the hands of otherwise fundamentally orthodox Governments in the same direction.

## (11) THE "GOLD CLAUSE" AFFAIR

The development of the gold-clause controversy in the United States was followed with keen interest in Europe. When in June 1933 Congress passed the law invalidating gold clauses in loan contracts, it was received with mixed feelings on this side. Everybody agreed that the decision amounted to an act of repudiation. This fact was welcomed by many people on the ground that it would provide an excuse for the repudiation of European war debts to the United States. Needless to say, the war-debt payments would have been defaulted upon in any case; in fact most debtor countries had already committed default before President Roosevelt decided to repudiate the gold clause. At the same time, it is probable that that act made it easier for Great Britain and some other debtors to make up their minds to suspend the payment of annuities. On the other hand, much concern was caused by the possibility of the example being followed by commercial debtors all over the world. It was feared that, encouraged by the repudiation of the gold clause, a number of debtor countries would be inclined to introduce arbitrary changes in their own loan contracts. In fact, during the second half of 1933 and during 1934 there were a series of new defaults, but it is difficult to form an opinion as to how far the mere effect of the repudiation of the gold clause was responsible for them. It is equally difficult to express an opinion as to whether on balance Europe was a gainer or a loser as a result of the invalidation of the gold clause.

Opinion in Europe is practically unanimous that, given the fact of the suspension of the gold standard and of the depreciation of the dollar, the abolition of the gold clause was inevitable. Arguments that the act was unconstitutional failed to create any profound impression over here. It was generally realised that the application of the gold clause would have created impossible conditions in the United States. Though in orthodox quarters hopes were entertained that the difficulties thus created would induce President Roosevelt to revalue the dollar, if not actually at its old parity, certainly well above its present gold value, most people realised the absurdity of such hopes. Even those who strongly condemned President Roosevelt's action of depreciating and devaluing the dollar realised that, having done so, he could not "unscramble the eggs". The contention that the United States Government had no right under the constitution to interfere with the value of its currency was considered highly unconvincing. The view is held that a Government backed up by the majority of its Parliament and by the majority of the electorate is entitled to make any changes it considers advisable. Considering that its right to decide upon war and peace has never been called in question, it is difficult to see how its right to alter the value of the monetary unit and to alter contracts can be challenged.

If the gold-clause controversy in the United States had a profound and lasting effect upon European opinion, it was in a somewhat unexpected direction.

It drew attention to the rigid legalism and one-sidedness of the moral code which had developed in all modern countries in the interest of creditors and at the expense of debtors. Until the notorious "gold-clause action" before the Washington Supreme Court, it had not been adequately realised how essentially legal and moral principles which had come to be regarded as fundamental had favoured creditors during a period of falling prices. By the rigid application of the rule that creditors were entitled to be paid in the monetary unit of the contracts, irrespective of changes in the commodity value of that monetary unit, free gifts had been showered upon creditors at the expense of debtors during the last five years or so. It was considered a matter of course that the same number of monetary units should be payable even though its real value had doubled in the meantime. Creditors considered themselves fully entitled to this surplus and their spokesmen were outraged if they were deprived of part of this unearned surplus by the devaluation of a currency. President Roosevelt, through his attitude towards the gold clause, laid down the doctrine that a Government was entitled to relieve the excessive burden of debtors by depreciating its currency if that burden threatened to become unbearable as a result of a rise in the commodity value of the monetary unit.

His example has already found followers among other first-rate countries. It is doubtful whether the Italian, German, and Belgian Governments would have had the moral courage to carry out forced conversions, even under the disguise of voluntary conversion offers, but for the example of the United States. Even France has derived inspiration from

President Roosevelt's attitude towards the legality of debt contracts. In July 1935 M. Laval reduced by decree the interest on all public debt and on certain categories of private debt to the extent of 10 per cent. Such an action would have been unthinkable before President Roosevelt had set an example.

In the past it had been the rule for honest debtors to pay twenty shillings in the pound until they collapsed under the burden of the payment. The precedent created by the gold-clause decision constituted an important departure from this practice. The United States Government as such was still solvent when President Roosevelt's gold-clause decision, endorsed by Congress, changed the terms of loan contracts in favour of the debtor. There can be no doubt, however, that the enforcement of the letter of the contract would have led to insolvency. Evidently it was not to the interest of the creditors themselves that their debtors should bleed to death in an attempt to meet their liabilities. Rather than be paid twenty shillings in the pound for a while and then nothing, a sensible creditor prefers to receive fifteen shillings or less, as the additional feeling of security makes up for his loss of income. In the case of the United States in 1933, there was no question of reducing payments from twenty shillings to fifteen shillings in the pound, but merely of preventing an increase of payments to thirty shillings or more. When the burden of a debt payment increases far beyond the amount it represented at the time of its conclusion, debtors have a strong moral claim for the scaling down of that burden. Hitherto a rigid conception of legalism had prevented all reputable debtors from obtaining recognition of this moral claim.

President Roosevelt's great merit lies in the fact that he dealt a heavy blow to this legalistic conception.

### (12) SUMMARY

Taking everything into account, there can be no doubt that President Roosevelt has produced a more profound influence upon Europe than any other statesman since the war, with the possible exceptions of Signor Mussolini and Lenin. While these two statesmen influenced Europe in the political sphere, President Roosevelt has revolutionised our conceptions in many respects in the economic sphere. Through his unorthodox example he has compelled us to revise many well-established doctrines. Although his influence upon the material economic situation in Europe has been immense, in the long run it will doubtless be overshadowed by his influence upon economic policies and conceptions.

President Roosevelt's material influence on Europe may be summarised in the following points:

(1) The undervaluation of the dollar affected adversely the competitive capacity of British and other European export trade.

(2) By depreciating the dollar, he compelled Great Britain and the rest of the Sterling Bloc to depreciate their currencies.

(3) As a result of his efforts to raise commodity prices in the United States, world prices underwent a moderate rise.

(4) The depreciation of the dollar and the subsequent depreciation of sterling compelled the countries of the Gold Bloc to continue to deflate.

(5) President Roosevelt's policy has thus resulted

in an improvement of conditions within the Sterling Bloc and a further deterioration of conditions within the Gold Bloc.

The following is a summary of the moral effect of President Roosevelt's policy upon Europe:

(1) He created an important precedent by suspending the gold standard as a matter of expediency before it became technically inevitable.

(2) He created a precedent by causing deliberately a depreciation of the national currency in the interest of the general economic welfare of the nation.

(3) He indicated the possibility of a reasonable and acceptable compromise with bimetallism.

(4) He drew attention to the importance of raising wages in accordance with higher prices and higher profits in the interest of steady prosperity.

(5) He provided an example of extensive State interference with economic life by a non-Communist and non Fascist Government.

(6) He provided an example of a policy of public works on a gigantic scale.

(7) He established the right of Governments to revise the terms of loan contracts in an extreme situation.

It is possible, and in the author's opinion even probable, that the financial and economic system of the world, when it emerges from the present period of depression, will be affected permanently by President Roosevelt's influence. If and when the gold standard is restored, it will probably be based on the principle that the Governments reserve the right to suspend it or to modify the parities as a matter of expediency in the case of persistent pressure. It is most unlikely that the world will again allow itself to drift into a situation in which the rigid maintenance of badly fixed gold parities imposes extreme suffering upon mankind. The gold standard of the future will have to be based upon the understanding that if and when the sacrifices involved in the defence of the existing parities become excessive, the Governments should have the right to take the line of least resistance. In this respect, President Roosevelt's policy of suspending the gold standard and of causing the dollar deliberately to depreciate will have determined a fundamental principle of the monetary system of the future. It is less certain whether his attitude towards silver will produce a lasting effect, but it is conceivable that statesmen anxious to avoid the recurrence of monetary scarcity will play for safety by including silver to a limited degree, without at the same time accepting full bimetallism.

In the sphere of economic policy it seems to the author highly probably that the influence of the principles of the New Deal will survive the emergency that rendered their application necessary. The distribution of purchasing power, which in the past was allowed to take care of itself, will in future be subject to much attention, and in the long run the tendency towards economic planning has undoubtedly come to stay. It is equally probable that the rule of supplementing private initiative by public works will in future be applied extensively. Last but by no means least, the outcome of the gold-clause action will influence the world towards taking a more realistic view of the problem of debts in future.

America has given a powerful lead to Europe. Its exact significance and the extent of its probable effects cannot as yet be foreseen. After all, President Roosevelt is still far from having concluded his work. He is quite capable of jumping new surprises at any moment upon Europe. Indeed, the possibility of changes in his policy constitutes one of the main sources of uncertainty. Will he drift towards a more extreme form of radicalism, or will he succumb to orthodox influences? Will he abandon his boldest schemes for the sake of terminating his conflict with the business community, or will he throw in his lot with labour organisations? Will he decide to stabilise the dollar definitely in the near future, or will he devalue it once more? Will he return to the gold standard, or will he adopt one of the many monetary reform proposals? Will he plunge himself whole-heartedly into inflation, or will he follow the more conservative advice of his Treasury officials? Will he force Great Britain to depreciate sterling further, or will he be forced to devalue further by a fall of sterling? Will he drive the members of the Gold Bloc off the gold standard, or will he assist them in their effort to retain their parities? These and innumerable other questions await answers, and in the meantime it would be rash to commit oneself to too definite conclusions about the effects of his policy upon Europe.

One thing, however, is certain. Even if his experiment were to fail completely, or even if he were to back out of it before its final results could be ascertained, he would have succeeded in stirring up Europe to reconsider doctrines which in the past were regarded as foregone conclusions. He has certainly made it impossible for Europe to return to the groove from which she was ejected by the world crisis. He has started an avalanche which will proceed on its way no matter what happens to its originator.

# M. VAN ZEELAND THE BANKER-PREMIER

## (1) BELGIUM AND DEFLATION

IN an address delivered before the Cornhill Club on "Bankers and Deflation" (a summary of which appears in this volume), the author raised the question of whether bankers as such are necessarily orthodox deflationists. He supported the view that this is not necessarily the case. His opinion received striking confirmation from the example of the new Belgian banker-premier, M. Van Zeeland. At a time when bankers are frequently accused of being reactionary, when they are represented by their opponents as the arch-enemies of progress, it is gratifying to be able to point to M. Van Zeeland's example to prove that bankers can be progressive in their attitude towards monetary, financial, and economic policy.

To appreciate the significance of the rôle M. Van Zeeland played it is necessary to give a summary of the events which led to his appointment as Prime Minister and head of a Government of National Union. During the three years that preceded the devaluation of the belga Belgium suffered intensely as a result of the deflationary policy pursued by her Governments. Her currency was grossly overvalued, and this handicapped Belgian export trade to a large degree. Belgium is dependent upon her foreign trade to a relatively larger extent than any other country, owing to her predominantly industrial character and the high density of her population. In order to be able to feed the nation and to provide raw materials for her industries it was of vital importance to maintain exports at a relatively high figure. There were two alternative ways of attaining this end. The one was to pursue a ruthless deflationary policy in order to reduce costs sufficiently to enable Belgian goods to find markets abroad. The other was to eliminate the obstacle to export trade by devaluing the currency or by allowing it to depreciate. For over three years the Belgian Governments persistently pursued the first course. There was a deflationary drive which forced costs down to a sufficient extent to make it possible for Belgium to export steel even to Great Britain, notwithstanding the British import duties and the depreciation of sterling.

## (2) THE CRISIS OF MARCH 1935

Needless to say, the nation suffered intensely through the deflationary drive and there was a growing discontent with the official monetary policy. Moreover, the Belgian public realised to an increasing degree that, notwithstanding the deflationary efforts, the devaluation of the belga was a mere question of time. Consequently, there was a persistent outflow of capital which from time to time assumed spectacular dimensions. At the beginning of March 1935, the voices demanding a change in the monetary policy were becoming louder. The Government of M. Theunis was, however, adamant in its pursuance of a deflationary policy. This in spite of the fact that at the time even in France the authorities declared themselves against any further deflation, and since the beginning of 1935 had been endeavouring to adopt a policy of cheap money leading to reflation.

During the second week of March, the flight of capital from Belgium began to assume the characteristics of a landslide. The National Bank of Belgium maintained the stability of the belga by selling gold, thereby weakening its technical position to a large degree. At the same time the forward exchange, which received no official support, went to a fantastic discount. Judging by the extent of the loss of gold it was obvious that should the drain continue on the same scale Belgium would be forced off gold within a few weeks.

M. Theunis made a desperate effort to obtain assistance from France in the form of the admission of an increased quantity of Belgian goods, but came back from his Paris visit empty-handed. Notwithstanding this, a member of his Government had the audacity to announce to the world, "The belga is saved". The events of the subsequent fortnight proved how far it is safe to rely upon such official reassuring statements in matters of currency stability.

On his return to Brussels, M. Theunis inaugurated a series of desperate measures for the defence of the belga. Drastic exchange restrictions were introduced to stop the flight of capital, and preparations were made to launch out on another deflationary drive. When all this was done, suddenly and unexpectedly M. Theunis announced his resignation. This in spite of the fact that he had an adequate parliamentary majority and that only a few days earlier Parliament renewed his authority to defend the belga by decrees for another three months.

### (3) THE CABINET CRISIS

It is difficult to understand the reasons why M. Theunis left his post amidst extreme emergency. The belga was subject to a violent speculative attack in addition to the effects of the flight of Belgian capital. The banking situation was becoming increasingly dangerous, owing to the wholesale withdrawals of deposits in connection with the flight from the belga. In the course of a few weeks, deposits to the amount of about 800 million belgas were withdrawn from the banks. The atmosphere was growing increasingly panicky and the threat of a major disaster was in the air. In such circumstances a Prime Minister who throws down his office without being forced to do so lays himself open to well-deserved criticism. Obviously a Cabinet crisis was the worst possible thing that could happen at that moment. It inevitably aggravated the panic, especially as, owing to the great difficulties of forming another Government, the Cabinet crisis was bound to be protracted.

For nearly a week amidst a crisis of first-rate magnitude Belgium was without a Government. The outgoing Ministers continued in office but confined themselves to routine measures. There was nobody to tackle the crisis of increasing gravity. The politicians who were requested by the King to form a new Government declined the task one after the other. Indeed, it was anything but enviable to assume responsibility either for the defence of the belga with the aid of unpopular measures or for its devaluation.

While the politicians were unable to find a way out of the crisis, the belga worked out its own solution. In face of the heavy selling pressure the National Bank

M

had to relax its support and the result was a sharp depreciation of the belga. Although the official rates of exchange in Brussels were maintained within gold points, in reality the belga went to a heavy discount in foreign centres. It thus created a *fait accompli*. And yet none of the political leaders was prepared to assume responsibility for giving official recognition to what had already become a fact.

### (4) M. VAN ZEELAND'S MISSION

It was at this moment that the King decided to call upon M. Van Zeeland to form a Government. The choice was bold, since the popularity of bankers in Belgium was none too great. If in spite of this the King invited the Deputy Governor of the National Bank of Belgium to form a Cabinet, it was because he realised that M. Van Zeeland was the right man for tackling the extremely difficult and dangerous situation. Although for a short while he held a Cabinet post in the Government of M. de Brockeville last year, M. Van Zeeland was essentially non-political. He did not concern himself about the probable effects of his measures upon the electorate. Being primarily a banker, he was capable of taking a quick decision and following it up by action when politicians would have hesitated and debated while the danger was growing.

On assuming office amidst a crisis, his position was somewhat similar to that of the British National Government in 1931 or that of President Roosevelt in 1933. The National Government made a desperate effort to save the pound and only yielded to pressure after having exhausted all its resources. It took President Roosevelt six weeks to make up his mind to allow

the dollar to depreciate. M. Van Zeeland's decision was
ready the moment he assumed office and three days
later he announced his plans. In less than a week
they were put into practice. His efficiency in dealing with the situation in such a short time deserves
the highest praise. The results provide full justification of his action.

## (5) DEVALUATION OF THE BELGA

M. Van Zeeland duly realised that any further resistance to the adverse pressure on the belga was futile.
The National Bank could not afford much longer to
spend hundreds of millions week after week in trying
to bolster up the exchange. In any case, when M. Van
Zeeland took over the reins the belga was already
depreciated, and it would have been a hopeless task to
try to unscramble the eggs. Whoever stepped into the
inheritance of M. Theunis had no alternative but to
accept the *fait accompli*. That is why the heads of the
various political parties were not prepared to take over
the heritage of M. Theunis. It was left to a banker
with no political allegiance and no political ambitions
to face realities. The moment M. Van Zeeland decided
to undertake the task of forming a Cabinet, he made
up his mind to devalue the belga. Indeed, on March 29
he announced his decision to that effect, and on March
31, after having obtained the approval of his policy
from Parliament, he issued a decree devaluing the belga
by 28 per cent.

The result of the step was a complete cessation
of the Belgian crisis overnight. The withdrawals of
deposits from the banks ceased instantaneously. In
fact, deposits began to pour back to the banks. The

decline in the gold reserve of the National Bank came to an end and was followed by a spectacular rise in the gold stock. At its new level, the belga inspired complete confidence. Those who a week before were doing their utmost to send their capital abroad began to repatriate their funds. During the first week after the devaluation, the National Bank recovered £14 million of its lost gold. Such was the confidence in the devalued belga that the forward exchange went immediately to a premium in relation to sterling, and has remained at a premium ever since. In Paris the belga has been at a premium most of the time, and occasionally it has been profitable to send gold from Paris to Brussels.

During the months that have followed devaluation, Belgium has become a refuge for foreign funds. Not only has the National Bank been able to recover all the gold lost prior to the devaluation, but the influx after April 1 exceeded the earlier efflux. French, Dutch, Swiss, and other foreign capital sought refuge in Belgium. The belga inspired confidence for the simple reason that it had had its depreciation while the gold currencies were yet to have theirs. Many of those who wanted to send their funds abroad from the Gold Bloc preferred to send them to Brussels rather than to London or New York because the belga was officially re-stabilised, while sterling was fluctuating and the dollar was only provisionally stabilised. Indeed, the influx of foreign funds assumed such dimensions as to threaten to cause an *embarras de richesse*. The National Bank has, however, taken steps to make it possible for refugee gold to leave the country easily without disturbing the monetary equilibrium of Belgium. After the middle of June, there was, in fact, a tendency for the return of some of the foreign funds that had taken refuge in Brussels, and the National Bank lost some of its newly acquired gold and foreign exchange. Notwithstanding this, its position remained stronger than before the crisis.

Had M. Van Zeeland not done anything else than assume responsibility for the devaluation of the belga he would have earned the gratitude of his nation. As a matter of fact, he has done and is doing a great deal more. Inspired by President Roosevelt's example, whose policy and methods he has had the opportunity of studying carefully, M. Van Zeeland has taken steps to secure for his country the maximum advantage from the devaluation. Those who imagined that the devaluation would open the door to inflationary profiteering reckoned without him. In order to minimise the disadvantages of the rise in commodity prices he did not hesitate to intervene in private business. Indeed, he even incurred the wrath of his former fellow-bankers by insisting upon the institution of a system of official inspection of the banks.

As a result of the unconventional policy he pursued, M. Van Zeeland has made many enemies. Indeed, in Belgium a substantial section of opinion, antagonised by the bold and unconventional policy he has followed, has been at pains to criticise him, to minimise the results of his efforts, and even to undermine his work by attacks on Government securities and the belga. These mischievous attempts have, however, been of no avail. While it is yet premature to form a definite judgment about the results of M. Van Zeeland's economic policy, it is certain that he saved his country from a financial and economic disaster of first-rate magnitude. If only his example would inspire the statesmen of the Gold Bloc who seem to attach more importance to the defence of a monetary doctrine than to the welfare of their countries, the international monetary problem would soon be well on its way towards a solution.

# THIS "GREAT" DEPRESSION

*Sir Pierce:* "I am sorry the terrible experience of this war—the greatest war ever fought—has taught you no better, O'Flaherty."

*O'Flaherty:* "I don't know about its being a great war, sir. It's a big war; but that's not the same thing."

G. B. SHAW, O'Flaherty, V.C.

## (1) "GREAT" WAR OR "BIG" WAR?

WAS the war of 1914–1918 a great war or merely a big war? Most people never give a thought to this question. It does not occur to them that there is a difference between the two. Even Bernard Shaw's hero, having made this fine point of distinction, switches over to discuss the relation between Irish landlords and tenants instead of making it plain what he meant when saying that the war was big but not great and why he meant whatever he did mean. And yet the remark Shaw put into the mouth of the Irish sergeant contains a profound truth that is well worth exploring. Presumably, when his General talked in an awe-struck tone about the great war—"the greatest war ever fought"—he, like so many others, was under the spell of the statistics of the war. Doubtless the war of 1914–1918 produced record figures, the sizes of armies, the number of their guns, of dead and wounded, ships sunk, property destroyed, and money spent in the course of hostilities. But does this in itself justify the epithet "great"? Bernard Shaw and his hero did not think so. They just instinctively felt that, notwithstanding its staggering dimensions and astronomic figures, the war of 1914–1918 did not possess the characteristics which would have justified calling it great. Greatness implies something more than large figures.

If the war of 1914–1918 had been "the war to end war", a war which created "a world fit for heroes to live in", then there would have been every justification for calling it a Great War, irrespective of its statistics. In 1918, when Bernard Shaw's war-time play was written, there were many people who entertained such hopes. Bernard Shaw was not amongst them, and unfortunately events have proved that he was right. To-day nobody but a few incorrigible dreamers who are out of touch with realities would dare to hope that the war of 1914–1918 was the last war, and not even they would dare to claim that this depression-ridden world, which is preparing for the next war before it has recovered from the wounds of the last, is a world "fit for heroes to live in". The war, it is true, liberated millions of people from the oppression of foreign nations or of their own rulers, but placed other millions under oppression at least as ruthless as that which prevailed before 1914. Such changes as have taken place in consequence of the war are largely if not exclusively for the worse. And yet, people persist in calling it a "great" war, although in reality it was merely a big war, which, in the words of O'Flaherty, "is not the same thing".

## (2) "GREAT" DEPRESSION OR "BIG" DEPRESSION?

The same distinction must necessarily arise regarding the depression of 1929–193? (or possibly, 194?).

Is the depression the world is suffering from a great depression or merely a big depression? Many people —amongst them Professor Lionel Robbins, as the title of his book implies—think it is a great depression. Bernard Shaw's character, impressed by the statistics of the war, mistakes bigness for greatness; is Professor Robbins not guilty of the same error? In granting the depression the epithet "great", was he not unduly impressed by the unprecedented figures of unemployment, bank failures, the drop in foreign trade returns? He is by no means alone in thinking that he has discovered the elements of greatness in the phenomenon the world has been witnessing during the last six years. Is it not high time that another O'Flaherty raised the question of whether the present world depression is really great or simply big?

Astronomic figures do not in themselves make for a great depression any more than they make for a great war. We have indicated the conditions in which it would have been justifiable to call the war of 1914–1918 great. The conditions which would justify calling the present depression great are not altogether dissimilar. If it is "a depression to end depression", and if its result is the creation of "a world fit for workers to live in", it is impossible to begrudge it the epithet "great". If the depression were the inevitable transition period between two world systems, and if the system which emerged from it were different from, and better than, the one that preceded it, then, and only then, it would unquestionably contain the elements of greatness. If, however, the outcome of the depression proves to be as disappointing as that of the war, which merely shifted the burden of tyranny to other shoulders and created a prolonged armistice between two wars, then it would be paying the depression an entirely undeserved compliment to call it great.

### (3) LESSONS OF THE DEPRESSION

The French Revolution of 1789 deserves to be called great, since it led the way through bloodshed and immense suffering to the recognition of human rights and to an improvement in the conditions of mankind. The war of 1914–1918 cannot claim to have produced any such results. Will the ultimate balance-sheet of the present depression show on the credit side a permanent betterment of the system? Will it carry one step further the results of the Great Revolution by securing the right of human beings to decent conditions of existence? There seems to be a strong trend working in that direction. The depression has important lessons to teach, if only mankind were willing to learn.

The experience of the last few years has made it evident that a state of fundamental disequilibrium exists, owing to the excessive burden of fictitious capital and owing to the discrepancy between prices and exchanges in various countries. Unless and until this legacy of the *ancien régime* is liquidated, mankind cannot hope for lasting stability, let alone prosperity. If the depression is to justify its claim to greatness, it will have to liquidate this legacy. And yet the orthodox school, while generously advancing that epithet, is doing its utmost to prevent the depression from resulting in the liquidation of the various disequilibria. If Professor Robbins and those who think like him had their way, currencies would be stabilised to-day rather than to-morrow and at around their existing level, the gold currencies retaining their overvalued level. Such a stabilisation would perpetuate international disequilibrium and also the disequilibrium between fictitious wealth and real wealth. The period that would follow stabilisation in such circumstances would be characterised by a struggle to maintain stability in spite of the lack of equilibrium. The energies of the nations, which would otherwise be available for the progress of production and the improvement of the standard of living, would be exhausted in this futile struggle. The immense burden of fictitious capital would continue to constitute a millstone round the neck of mankind and the overvaluation of certain currencies would continue heavily to penalise certain nations, without in the long run benefiting others. It is difficult to discover any greatness in a depression leading to no better results.

## (4) AIMS OF THE ORTHODOX SCHOOL

Many of those who believed that the war of 1914–1918 was a great war based their belief merely on statistics. Others, however, based it on the idealistic hopes that it would fundamentally transform the world and that the change would be for the better. Does Professor Robbins and the school of thought he represents entertain such hopes? The answer is most emphatically in the negative. All the *laissez-faire* economists hope for and work for is to see the return of the system that operated in the olden days. To their mind, the present depression should not be "a depression to end depression". On the contrary, they pray for the return of the state of affairs in which cyclic crises are an integral part of the system and in which the progress of mankind is hampered by the measures that have to be taken for the mitigation of these crises. There are, in fact, extremists who think it better for the world to suffer from perpetual if mitigated depression on the basis of *laissez-faire* than to prosper on the basis of planning and intervention.

If the orthodox school had its way, the world would be made to return to conditions in which producers and traders could live up to the sacred principle of "everybody for himself and the survival of the fittest". They would be at liberty to use and abuse their means of production to their heart's desire; to exploit their workmen or their clients within the letter of the law; to work against public interests through selfish greed or through sheer ignorance. The world would remain the paradise of the Hatrys and Kreugers, the inevitable products of the *laissez-faire* system. It is indeed difficult to discover anything in such a result which would justify attributing greatness to the depression which led to it.

### (5) HOPES AND FEARS

It remains to be seen whether the outcome of the depression will be as negative as is desired by the orthodox school, and whether the sacrifices, like those of the last war, will thus be wasted. There is just a hope that the lessons of the depression may not have been altogether lost, that they may have made the world realise the necessity for fundamental changes. It is possible that, should the depression continue, it may lead to the liquidation of excessive fictitious wealth, whether through the adequate depreciation of currencies, the arbitrary or voluntary reduction of interest rates, or the creation of conditions in which an increase of production might be able to offset the disequilibrium between fictitious capital and real wealth. It is possible that in the absence of premature stabilisation currencies will eventually be stabilised in circumstances which will reduce to a minimum international disequilibrium. It is possible that, having learnt from the experience of the last few years, the freedom of individuals to commit blunders or make mischief by their economic activities will be curtailed and the anarchy of *laissez-faire* production will give way to a rational planned system It is possible that under the new system monetary stability will be regarded as a mere means to an end, while the end itself will be the progress and welfare of mankind; that, thanks to the application of economic planning combined with an unorthodox conception of monetary policy, mankind may at last be in a position to enjoy the full benefit of technical progress. Then, and then only, it would be fully justifiable to speak of the Great Depression.

If, on the other hand, the world fails to learn the dearly paid lessons of the last six years, and, after having caught a glimpse of the Land of Promise, relapses into the pettiness and meanness of *laissez-faire*, into the cult of selfishness and profit-worship, then we can only say with O'Flaherty: "I don't know about its being a great depression; it's a big depression, but that's not the same thing". And we may also remark with Sir Pierce: "I am sorry the terrible experience of this depression has taught you no better!"

# CONSISTENT DEFLATION

## (1) A NEW MONETARY POLICY

A NEW type of monetary policy—indeed, a new monetary system—has recently made its appearance. While the experts were debating, the statesmen of the Gold Bloc have evolved a new system without any theoretical background. For some time the system did not even have a name, but in the course of the debates in the Dutch Parliament in July 1935 it became known under the name of "consistent deflation".

In the past, both inflation and deflation were essentially irregular and haphazard movements. The fluctuation of various wholesale prices, retail prices, rents, and other items in the cost of living differed from each other widely, while there were certain items such as interest on debt and other fixed charges which remained unaffected by inflation and deflation. According to the new idea, deflation has to be carried through consistently in every sphere, that is, if for the sake of the defence of the gold parity of a currency public expenditure has to be cut, similar reductions are to be made in every direction, so as to adjust various items in the cost of living and fixed charges to the lower level.

The originator of this new system was Signor Mussolini. As early as 1931 he carried through an all-round cut in Civil Service salaries, and to make the sacrifice more bearable, he also ordered the reduction of rents and certain other items of the cost of living. Thanks to his dictatorial power, and to the discipline

of the Italian nation, he was well in a position to
carry out such a drastic and hitherto unprecedented
intervention in economic life. He repeated the same
all-round cut in 1934. During the same year, independently of these cuts, he reduced charges on Government, municipal, and mortgage loans by the encouragement of "voluntary" conversion operations which
were. in fact if not in law, forced conversions.

### (2) M. LAVAL'S MEASURES

For a long time it was believed that while a dictator
in a Fascist State was in a position to adopt such
measures, it was unthinkable under a system of Parliamentary democracy. The events of the last few weeks
have proved, however, that this is by no means the
case. In connection with his economy measures, M.
Laval adopted the same system. In fact, he went even
further, for, in addition to cutting rents and certain
items of the cost of living by decree, he also ordered the
reduction of interest on public and private indebtedness to the extent of 10 per cent. He did not take
the trouble to disguise this reduction under the pre-
tence of voluntary conversions. It was presented as
the logical outcome of the necessity for deflationary
measures in defence of the franc.

Soon after the publication of M. Laval's measures,
another democratic state resorted to the same system.
Dr. Colijn in attempting to balance the Dutch Budget
linked up his economy measures with reductions in the
interest on mortgage loans and other similar cuts.
Although the fate of his proposals after the reconstruction of his Cabinet remains at the time of writing uncertain, it appears that part of the opposition parties

criticise his measures on the ground that they do not go far enough. It is suggested that he should go a step further by cutting down not only the interest but also the principal of mortgage debts.

As is so often the case, practical developments have got ahead of theory. Indeed, theoretical economists are for the most part not even aware as yet that they are confronted with a new system. They regard the measures taken in Italy and France and those proposed in Holland as mere drastic emergency measures, and do not as yet realise they have a philosophy behind them. In their excuse it is fair to add that in all probability the statesmen and their expert advisers responsible for the elaboration of the measures are equally oblivious of the fact that what they have done is to bring into existence an entirely new monetary system. In this respect they are in a similar position to that of Christopher Columbus who when reaching the West Indies did not realise that he had discovered a new continent. Even the Dutch parliamentarians who had a heated debate over the idea of "consistent deflation" did not appear to be aware of the true significance of this innovation.

## (3) INADEQUATE CONSISTENCY

It is, of course, conceivable that, since the new system was brought into existence by the pressure on overvalued currencies, once this pressure has ceased the system will also be dropped. There is, however, a chance that, once the system has been adopted, a school of thought will develop which will consider it of permanent value. In its present form it presents, needless to say, innumerable anomalies and inconveniencies.

Although it is called "consistent", it is in reality far from being so. In order to be consistent it should cover every section of economic life, and should operate both in an upward and downward direction. Thus, if there is a rise or fall in commodity prices by, say, 10 per cent, every kind of retail price and other item of the cost of living, fixed charges, etc., should be made to move to a corresponding degree. In practice, such a system would, needless to say, meet with considerable difficulties. It is, for instance, unthinkable to carry out a 10 per cent increase or reduction in tram fares. For such minor items, the adjustment can only be approximate. In any case, even if consistent deflation or inflation is carried to its logical conclusion, it does not remove the iniquities caused by fluctuating prices. If an individual pays his rent on June 25 and receives a half-yearly interest payment on July 1, and between the two dates an all-round cut has been carried through, he will be definitely a loser on balance. Apart from considerations of equity, the system has serious practical disadvantages in that it would necessitate frequent changes in prices and charges which under the existing system remain stable for long periods. For the financially uneducated classes these changes would be highly confusing.

## (4) PRACTICAL ASPECTS

Let us now consider the immediate practical aspects of the new system. Will its application be able to save the gold currencies? Will consistent deflation provide an alternative to devaluation?

Let us take the example of France. It is possible that by forcing a reduction in the cost of living the

N

budgetary cuts may have been made less unbearable. This is, in fact, probably the reason why they did not meet with more violent opposition. As, however, deflation has not been carried through in every direction, those who suffered the cuts are on balance worse off than they were before. If the cuts are to be repeated, their position might easily become unbearable. And the chances are that the cuts will have to be repeated. Judging from past experience, it may be taken for granted that all-round cuts in Government expenditure, interest, etc., inevitably lead to a fall in revenue. Before very long the Budget will once again be unbalanced, and to meet the deficit the cuts will have to be repeated. As certain items such as expenditure on national defence cannot be touched, the cuts on the remaining items will have to be made all the heavier. The direct victims of the cuts will derive some compensation from a reduction in the cost of living, but once again it will be impossible to make the cuts operative in every sphere. There is bound to be growing discontent among victims of the cuts if the operation is repeated over and over again. What is more, it will establish a vicious circle in which cuts, reductions in the cost of living, lower purchasing power, falling prices and profits, and a decline in budgetary revenue will chase each other endlessly.

There is another danger-point which might upset the operation of the system. If carried far the application of consistent deflation not only to interest charges but also to capital burdens will be unavoidable. In fact, the Dutch opposition has already made proposals to that effect. In order to save debtors from insolvency, through the effects of deflation on their earnings and on the value of their assets, it would become necessary to reduce their liabilities. The result would be that the banks would suffer heavy losses. To be consistent, they would have to be indemnified through an extension of the cuts to deposits. Any such attempt would, however, result in wholesale withdrawals by depositors and would lead to financial collapse. Thus, in addition to leading to a budgetary deadlock, consistent deflation would also provoke a banking crisis.

## (5) WILL NEW SYSTEM SAVE GOLD BLOC?

Admittedly, consistent deflation will enable the countries of the Gold Bloc to prolong their resistance to devaluation. The fact that it enables their Governments to adjust debt charges downwards leads to a postponement of the moment when devaluation reduces itself to absurdity. It will, however, make no difference to the final outcome. Possibly consistent deflation may prolong the life of the gold currencies for six months or more, but it will not avert their ultimate fate.

By prolonging the futile struggle against devaluation, the new system renders a grave disservice to the countries directly concerned and to the world in general. On the other hand, it has a great compensating advantage. It tends to reduce the excessive burden of fictitious wealth. The experience of Great Britain during the last three years has proved that, notwithstanding the Government's policy of cheap money, it is a long and difficult process to arrive at a reduction of the interest burden by normal means. Indeed, after promising progress in the right direction, the decline in the yield of Government securities has come to a halt, while progress in the decline of mortgage and other interest charges has been quite unsatisfactory. Even if conversion to a lower basis were practicable, the existence of long-term contracts would prevent debtors from taking advantage of its possibilities. It is evident that, in order to reduce the burden of dead-weight debt, Government intervention is indispensable. Until recently, a time-honoured conception of legality prevented the Governments of the first-rate countries from reducing the burden of public and private indebtedness by cutting interest rates. The gold-clause legislation of President Roosevelt was the first step towards overcoming this legalistic conception. It was followed by forced conversion operations under the disguise of voluntary conversions in Italy, Germany, and Belgium. The action of the French Government in directly reducing interest rates constituted an even more severe blow to legalism. It created a highly important precedent and indicated the way in which excessive interest burdens can be reduced. There still remains the problem of excessive capital burdens. Even if the adherents of consistent deflation do not dare to tackle this problem, the reduction of the interest burden in itself goes a long way towards reducing the disequilibrium between fictitious wealth and real wealth, a disequilibrium which has been largely responsible for all the world's troubles since the war.

# BANKERS AND DEFLATION *

## (1) CHARGES AGAINST BANKERS

THE object of my address is to examine the attitude of bankers towards a monetary policy of ruthless deflation. I shall try to answer the question, whether bankers as such are necessarily deflationists and whether it is to their interest that they should favour deflation. The question is of considerable importance at a time when the attitude of bankers towards political and economic problems is subject to much discussion and criticism. Ever since 1931, bankers have been the scapegoats of political propaganda. They have been accused of various offences such as political intrigues, a selfish and narrow policy towards British industries, reckless lending abroad, etc. Above all, they have been accused of being in favour of a monetary policy which aims at increasing the value of the monetary unit by causing the fall in commodity prices. Bankers are represented by political and financial radicals as being born deflationists. It is alleged that it is to the interest of bankers to increase the value of the monetary unit because, being moneylenders, they stand to benefit by it. Bankers are accused of being prepared to sacrifice the interest of producers in order to secure to themselves the benefit obtained through increasing the value of money by means of deflation.

Absurd as these charges may appear, it is a mistake

* Extracts from an address delivered at the monthly meeting of the Cornhill Club on February 13, 1935.

to ignore them; and yet, as far as I know, none of the leading personalities of the banking community have taken the trouble to answer adequately the charge of being in favour of a deflationary monetary policy for selfish considerations. There would have been ample opportunity to answer this charge in the various chairmen's speeches delivered during the last few years. In particular, the speeches of the chairmen of the Big Five this year dealing with the question of the nationalisation of the banks would have provided an excellent opportunity for refuting charges of deflationism. It would have served a much more useful purpose than merely to express disapproval of the idea of nationalisation of the banks and marshal various arguments against it. An emphatic denial of being in favour of a deflationary monetary policy would have gone further to counteract propaganda directed against the banks than any of the arguments put forward by the bankers.

### (2) THE CUNLIFFE REPORT

The meaning of the charge that bankers are incorrigible deflationists is twofold. In the first place, it is alleged that they use their influence to induce the authorities to pursue a deflationary monetary policy. In the second place, it is alleged that they lend themselves as the willing executors of this monetary policy by putting deflation into operation through credit restrictions. Let us examine how much truth, if any, there is in both charges. Doubtless in the past prominent bankers did not hesitate to express opinions favouring a deflationary monetary policy. To mention the best-known example, the deflationary monetary policy pursued by this country after the war, which was responsible for the overvaluation of sterling by stabilising it at its pre-war parity in 1925, followed the lines indicated by the Cunliffe Committee. Notwithstanding this, it would be unfair to put the whole blame for the mistaken policy upon the shoulders of the bankers who signed the Cunliffe reports or who in subsequent public utterances supported the policy of deflation. The Government has at the Treasury highly qualified experts of its own who can think for themselves and need not come to the City to borrow ideas. The work of the Cunliffe Committee, like that of most other departmental committees or Royal Commissions, consisted of providing detailed arguments in favour of a policy which the Government wanted in any case to pursue.

But even if banks were guilty of deflationism during that period, there are many mitigating circumstances in their favour. They could not be expected in 1920 to see things as we see them in 1935. To be able to predict the disastrous consequences of the deflationary policy adopted on their recommendation by the Government would have required a most uncanny foresight. It is true that several prominent theoretical and practical experts were opposed to the deflationary policy that led to the restoration of the pound to its pre-war value. But they were mostly right for the wrong reason. As things were between 1920 and 1925, it was not unreasonable to assume that the policy adopted by the Government was the right policy. It was not until the advent of the crisis that the full extent of the adverse consequences of a deflationary monetary policy could be adequately realised. Such an extent of deflation as the world experienced during the past five years is entirely without precedent in modern financial history.

## (3) LOSSES THROUGH DEFLATION

The mistake made by the bankers advocating deflation after the war cannot in all fairness be regarded as unpardonable. On the other hand, if, in spite of the experience of the last few years, they were to adopt a similar deflationary attitude in future, it would be absolutely unpardonable, for now we all know what deflation means, and there can be no excuse for being in favour of a policy which inflicts deliberately such heavy sacrifices and sufferings as the world has had to put up with since 1929.

Is it to the interest of bankers to advocate a deflationary monetary policy? The answer is most emphatically in the negative. They have nothing to gain and a great deal to lose as a result of deflation. The suggestion that the bankers, being moneylenders, stand to gain by the appreciation of the monetary unit through deflation is sheer nonsense. Bankers are not only lenders but also borrowers, so that whatever they would gain as lenders through the fall of commodity prices, they would lose as borrowers. The extent to which banks are affected by changes in the value of the monetary unit is confined to that part of their capital and reserves which exceeds the value of the premises and other property they own. In any case, this relatively small gain is more than offset by their losses through bad debts caused by deflation and through the fall in their profits. Admittedly, if extreme inflation such as was witnessed in Central Europe after the war wipes out the monetary unit, it reduces the capital and reserve of the banks, which may thus be deprived of part of their working capital. This was the case of banks in Germany and elsewhere. It is,

therefore, evidently to the interest of bankers to oppose
extreme inflation to the utmost. It is, however, a long
way from opposing extreme inflation to favouring
deflation. Indeed, it may well be asked whether, if the
choice lay between extreme inflation and deflation,
the former would not be the smaller evil for banks.
Even though banks have lost part of their working
capital through extreme inflation, hardly any of them
have failed in consequence. On the other hand, deflation brought with it a series of bank failures in
almost every country. The fall in commodity prices was
inevitably accompanied by the accumulation of large
amounts of bad debts, and the distrust inspired by the
heavy losses suffered by banks often led to a run of
depositors. Fortunately, in this country we had no
such experience during the last crisis. In spite of this,
the banks were evidently losers as a result of deflation.
They suffered heavy losses in the first instance through
the post-war deflation of 1920–1921, when the slump
in commodity prices resulted in huge frozen debts in
Lancashire and elsewhere. Thus, even though the deflation of 1920–1921 was carried out on the advice of
bankers, it can hardly be said that bankers benefited
by it. The extent to which banks suffered through the
crisis of the last few years is not known, but there can
be no doubt that it was considerable.

## (4) CENTRAL BANKS' ATTITUDE

In the circumstances, it is evidently absurd to
suggest that banks stand to gain by advocating a
deflationary monetary policy. There is indeed no
reason whatsoever why bankers as such should be in
favour of deflation, at any rate as far as joint-stock

banks and private banks are concerned. The position
may appear somewhat different as far as Central
Banks are concerned. It is conceivable that they might
consider it to their interest to favour a deflationary
monetary policy and that they would use all their
influence to induce the Government, which has the last
word in the matter, to adopt such a policy. After all, it
is their job to look after the stability of the currency,
and they may think it desirable to go to great lengths
to perform this function. In the light of the experience
of recent years, however, there is reason to hope that
even Central Bankers will become less deflationary in
future than they have been in the past. For it is now
evident that deflation cannot be carried on indefinitely.
In the past it was assumed that a currency could always
be saved from depreciation, provided that the monetary authorities were prepared to adopt a policy of
ruthless deflation. The experience of recent years has
proved that deflation may reach a limit beyond which
it cannot continue. After a certain stage, deflation
tends to set in motion factors which defeat its own
object. The inevitable consequence of prolonged deflation of a considerable degree is a large budgetary deficit,
and the difficulties of coping with the chronic deficit
lead to inflationary measures which reverse the trend.
Deflation cannot be carried on for ever even if the
Government and the country are prepared to do so. If,
as a result of a fall in prices and a depression in trade,
budgetary revenues decline, and if it is impossible to
reduce expenditure to a corresponding degree, the
Government may find it increasingly difficult to meet
the deficit by means of normal borrowing, and sooner
or later will have to fall back upon inflation. France
will inflate sooner or later, not because she will change

her monetary policy, but because deflation will reach a stage at which it will reduce itself *ad absurdum*. When as a result of inflation the franc has to be devalued, the French monetary authorities may well ask themselves whether it was worth their while to inflict upon the country such heavy sacrifices for the sake of defending the franc during the last few years. They may realise that if the adverse trend appears to be strong and persistent, it is not to the interest of Central Banks to resist it to the utmost by pursuing a deflationary monetary policy.

## (5) POLITICAL ASPECT

Apart from financial and economic considerations, it is contrary to the political interests of bankers in general, and Central Bankers in particular, to be in favour of a deflationary monetary policy. They could afford to be deflationary so long as public opinion did not adequately realise the consequences of such a policy. Having learnt from the experience of the last few years, the public now knows too much about deflation to put up with it. It is unthinkable that the policy pursued by the British Government after the war could be repeated without arousing a wave of indignation which would sweep away the Government and the party responsible for such a policy. The party which is opposed to deflation stands to gain many millions of votes at the next General Election. If bankers use their influence in favour of a deflationary policy, the anti-deflationary Government which will come into power will have the backing of public opinion in taking drastic measures to gain control over the banks. Evidently, it would be suicidal for bankers, in the circumstances, to support a policy favouring deflation. Nor would it be sufficient merely to keep silent on the subject. In the absence of authoritative denials, the conception popularised by skilful propaganda that bankers are as deflationist as they were in 1920 will be assumed to be correct by public opinion. It is to the interest of the banks, therefore, not only to abstain from taking up an attitude in favour of deflation, but to make it quite plain that they are against such a policy.

### (6) ECONOMISTS AND CREDIT RESTRICTIONS

The critics of the banks, in addition to stating that bankers use their influence in favour of deflation, also accuse them of lending themselves to be executors of deflationary monetary policy. As is well known, one of the most effective means by which deflation can be carried out is through credit restrictions. It is a ruthless method of counteracting a rising trend of commodity prices and forcing a decline of commodity prices. By curtailing credit banks are in a position to force their customers to throw their stocks on the market, thereby causing a fall in commodity prices. In many cases this leads to insolvencies, and the bankrupt stocks thus thrown on the market accentuate and accelerate the slump.

A great deal has been written by orthodox economists in favour of this method. In order to whitewash the policy of deflation through credit restrictions, the economists go so far as to make it appear a desirable process of "purging economic life from unwanted elements". They always talk about the failures which inevitably accompany credit restric-

tions on a large scale as the "elimination of weak and
unsound positions". They choose to remain pleasantly
vague as to what exactly they mean by "weak and
unsound positions". Do they mean enterprises which
are engaged in work that is of no social utility and
which, in fact, is actually harmful? Most certainly
not. To their mind, a company engaged in the manufacture of harmful drugs or in white slave traffic is
perfectly sound so long as it has an adequate cash
balance. On the other hand, an enterprise engaged in
the manufacture of surgical appliances which might
save life and reduce suffering is unsound if its cash
position happens to be weak at the moment of the
credit restriction. However useful it may be for the
welfare of mankind, orthodox economists rub their
hands with satisfaction if it fails, saying that "some
more weak and unsound positions have been liquidated". Do they mean by unsound enterprises, companies which in the long run are unable to pay their
way and commercially therefore have no *raison d'être*?
I doubt it. A company may be perfectly sound
commercially, but may happen to be overdrawn at
the moment when credit restrictions are applied and
may not be able to liquidate its stocks in good enough
time to meet the emergency. On the other hand,
another company may be thoroughly unsound commercially, but may possess at the time of credit
restriction sufficient liquid resources to weather the
storm. What orthodox economists mean when they
talk about credit restriction eliminating weak and
unsound positions is that they eliminate firms which
at the moment happen to be in an illiquid position.
They have not, however, the courage and the intel-
lectual honesty to say so. They deliberately convey

the impression when advocating credit restriction
that the failure of the firms who become the victims
of these measures is a process desirable for its own
sake, that the firms which fail are in reality superfluous and undesirable and that the world is better
off without them. Indeed, they seek to obtain approval
of their policy by false pretences.

### (7) BANKERS AND CREDIT RESTRICTIONS

Ignorant and malevolent people attribute a similar
attitude to bankers in matters of credit restriction.
They want us to believe that bankers are in favour of
deflating by cutting down credit, that they actually
enjoy doing so. It is amazing how anyone can possibly
believe such an absurdity. I can imagine how distaste-
ful it must be for branch managers to call in credits
from their valued customers without any specific
reason for doing so. The debtors are exactly as sound
as they were yesterday and yet they have to be called
upon to pay part or the whole of their overdraft according to instructions received from head office to
reduce the outstanding amount by such and such a
figure. Nor is it conceivable that the head office enjoys
sending out such instructions. It would not do so unless
it were compelled to do so by deflationary measures
taken by the monetary authorities which reduced the
basis for bank credits. It is not the branch managers
nor the head offices that are responsible for the cuts
they have to apply, but the official monetary policy.
Under the existing system banks have to maintain a
certain minimum cash ratio, and if the amount of their
deposits with the Central Bank is reduced through deflationary action on the part of the latter, they have

no choice but to adjust their outstanding credits to the change. It is, therefore, most unfair to suggest that bankers are deflationists because they lend themselves as executors of the official monetary policy. They lend themselves to that task with the utmost reluctance and it is decidedly not to their interest to do so.

If any bankers are responsible for deflationary credit restrictions, it is only those who control the policy of the Central Bank. Even their responsibility has become considerably reduced during recent years. In the past, the directors of the Bank of England were allowed a free hand within certain limits in determining the monetary policy of the country. The tendency is, however, for monetary policy to be directed to an increasing degree by the Treasury, and the Central Bank confines itself to executing the policy decided upon by the Government. Those bankers who are inclined to deplore this curtailment of their influence should be reminded that it is not only their influence but also their responsibility that is being reduced. I am convinced that the change is decidedly for the better as far as bankers are concerned. If in future unpopular monetary measures have to be taken, it will no longer be possible to put the blame on the wicked bankers.

# BANKERS AND STABILISATION

## (1) ATTITUDE OF CLEARING BANKS

ACCORDING to the popular belief, the London banking community as a whole is definitely in favour of immediate and unconditional stabilisation of sterling. This is the impression gained from the speeches and other public utterances of bankers. With few exceptions, bankers never miss an opportunity to emphasise in public the necessity of early stabilisation of sterling. The example of the chairmen of the Big Five, who since the war have adopted the habit of discussing in their annual addresses questions of monetary policy, has been followed by the heads of smaller banks, so that it is nowadays hardly possible to read a report of a bank meeting without discovering some reference to the necessity for immediate stabilisation. Also on the occasion of Lord Mayors' banquets, annual bankers' dinners, etc., most speakers do not fail to express their opinion that the Government should stabilise forthwith.

And yet banking opinion on the subject is not nearly as unanimous as would appear on the surface. Even among the chairmen of the Big Five there is one who has always been known for his radical views on monetary policy. It is true that, at the other extreme, leading clearing bankers are members of the Sound Currency Association and of the Friends of Economy Association. The fact remains, nevertheless, that the attitude of the heads of clearing banks is far from being unanimously in favour of immediate stabilisation. The number of directors and senior executive officials of the leading banks who are against immediate stabilisation is larger than most people realise. If in spite of this it hardly ever happens that well-known bankers express themselves against immediate stabilisation, it is because they are afraid of antagonising their chiefs or their colleagues or their clients. The personal experience of the author is that many bankers who would not think of committing themselves in public against an early stabilisation of sterling hold very strong views to that effect and do not hesitate to express them in private.

Is it to the interest of bankers that sterling should be stabilised immediately? As far as clearing banks are concerned, it is obvious that their prosperity depends mainly upon home trade, and only to a relatively small degree upon foreign trade. So long as home trade remains as prosperous as it is at present, the clearing banks are well in a position to earn a living in spite of low interest rates. Admittedly, from the point of view of their earning possibilities, it may appear on the surface desirable to witness an increase in interest rates, and since immediate stabilisation would in all probability entail a higher bank rate, some bankers may be inclined to advocate stabilisation from that point of view. The predominant majority of bankers in favour of stabilisation are not, however, prompted by such selfish considerations. They duly realise that their meat would be the poison of industrial and commercial firms, and that while higher interest rates might increase their margin of profit, they would certainly tend to reduce their turnover, and they would also increase their frozen assets.

## (2) ATTITUDE OF BANKING HOUSES

The position of banking houses is to a large extent different from that of joint-stock banks. The former depend to a very large extent upon earnings from foreign trade and international financial transactions. Since it is assumed that stabilisation should be followed by a revival of international trade and finance, financial houses are almost unanimous in demanding immediate stabilisation.

We may well ask, however, whether it is justifiable to take it for granted that stabilisation would lead to a revival of international trade and finance. All depends upon the conditions in which stabilisation takes place. If the currencies are stabilised in circumstances which tend to perpetuate the existing state of disequilibrium, it is not justifiable to expect a substantial and lasting increase in the volume of foreign trade and international financial business. The countries whose currencies remain overvalued will have to continue to defend their exchanges by means of restrictions and the rest of the world will have to follow their example. Moreover, stabilisation built upon disequilibrium would inspire distrust which in itself would go a long way towards preventing a true revival of international trade and finance. For this reason, those who believe that immediate stabilisation would bring back the pre-crisis prosperity of foreign business would be disappointed if their policy were to be tested in practice.

## (3) DOMESTIC BUSINESS INCREASING

Another question worth examining is whether banking houses really depend for their prosperity upon a revival of foreign operations. Doubtless since the contraction of foreign business they have been having a lean time, although the decline in the volume of acceptance credits is partly offset by the increase of the commissions they are in a position to charge. There is, however, nothing to take the place of their profits on international loan operations, which in existing conditions are practically non-existent. The remedy lies, however, to a very large extent in the hands of the banking houses themselves. Admittedly, there is at present not enough foreign business to go round. In face of this situation some of the banking houses spend their days in enforced idleness, which gives them ample time to complain about bad conditions and to pray for the return of the happy pre-crisis days. Other banking houses, however, employ their time more usefully. Instead of living on hopes of a revival of foreign business, they have been making serious efforts to increase their home business. Several acceptance houses and discount houses have made considerable efforts to popularise the use of the inland acceptance. In certain special branches these endeavours have been remarkably successful. To mention only one, instalment selling has provided useful material for the bill market. Experience has shown that, even amidst the depression of the last few years, the percentage of defaults on instalment business has been negligible. In any case, the bills bear the name of an instalment financing company of standing, so that the risk is further reduced. Given the existing conditions in home trade, it may be said that these bills are as safe and sound as any first-class foreign bills which are accepted and discounted in London.

Nor is it inevitable for the issuing departments

of banking houses to remain idle. It is true that
there are no foreign loans, but there is ample opportunity for them to take up sound domestic issues.
Before the crisis, industrial and other domestic issues
were largely left to the care of second-rate, third-rate,
and hundredth-rate issuing houses. The leading firms
were too busy issuing foreign loans to bother about
such transactions. Since the crisis, however, one leading house after another has discovered that a good
industrial or commercial issue may be just as profitable
for them as a foreign loan transaction. As a result, we
witness the flotation of domestic issues by banking
houses which in the past would never have thought of
taking an interest in such matters. They were compelled by sheer necessity to look for such new earning
possibilities, but once these were discovered, the banking houses found them a highly lucrative branch of
activity. The chances are that the later the revival
in foreign business takes place, the more banking
houses will benefit by the expansion of their home
business.

From this point of view alone it is against the interest
of the London banking community to hasten the
stabilisation of sterling, apart altogether from the fact
that if stabilisation were to take place in the existing
circumstances, it would not lead to a substantial and
lasting recovery in foreign business.

In laying too much stress upon their opinion in
favour of immediate stabilisation, bankers tend to
accentuate the conflict between the City and the rest
of the country. They convey the impression that the
banking community is in favour of stabilisation even
if it is highly detrimental to trade in general. They
provide useful material for those agitators who for

political purposes try to work up a feeling of hostility in the country against the City. This consideration alone should make it worth while for the banking community to reconsider its attitude towards immediate stabilisation.

# BANKERS AND INFLATION

## (1) EXTREME INFLATION CONDEMNED

THROUGHOUT the world at all times industrial and agricultural producers have been inclined to favour an inflationary monetary policy. On the other hand, the rentier and other classes with fixed incomes have been in favour of deflation. It would be interesting to examine the position of the banking community between the two extremes. While the interests of producers favouring inflation are as obvious as those of the classes with fixed incomes favouring deflation, it is not so evident where the interests of bankers lie. The public and even many bankers are inclined to take it for granted that it is the sacred duty of bankers to lead a crusade against inflation. In cartoons they are represented as the high priests of the cult of the golden calf. Their unpopularity in quarters favouring credit expansion has increased considerably in recent years when the adverse effects of credit restrictions on trade have become evident.

It goes without saying that bankers, like everybody else with common sense, are opposed to extreme inflation such as the world experienced during and immediately after the war. Apart from considerations of public interest, bankers stand to lose a great deal through excessive inflation. It is true that, since it results in a depreciation of their liabilities as well as of their assets, they are not likely to become insolvent through inflation. From this point of view, it is incomparably less harmful for banks than deflation. They stand to lose, however, in that their capital and reserves are likely to depreciate. During the period of extreme inflation, banks in Central Europe built themselves palaces and acquired art treasures so that their Board rooms and Directors' offices looked more like museums than banks. By adopting this policy, they succeeded in saving some of their resources from utter depreciation. Notwithstanding this, practically all banks in countries where inflation reached an advanced stage emerged from the crisis with their resources considerably reduced. Even in countries where inflation was checked before it reached an advanced stage, bankers were if anything losers rather than gainers from inflation.

## (2) EXCESSIVE CAUTION

It is, therefore, in the interest of bankers to oppose any policy which may lead to uncontrolled inflation. Many bankers, being over-cautious by the nature of their profession, are inclined to err on the safe side by opposing rigidly any policy of credit expansion for fear that it may develop into reckless inflation. Indeed, some of them, to be entirely on the safe side, are ardent supporters of deflation so as to remove every risk of inflation. They do not realise that, from their point of view, the remedy they are so keen on applying is incomparably worse than the disease they are trying to avoid.

While bankers have good reason to oppose advanced inflation and even relatively moderate uncontrolled inflation, situations may arise in which moderate inflation, kept well under control, is in accordance with their interest. In the United States, for instance, where prolonged deflation resulted in the wholesale bankruptcy of the banks' debtors, it was evidently in accordance with the interest of bankers that President Roosevelt should succeed in his policy of reflation. Indeed, that policy was undertaken largely for the sake of restoring the solvency of banks. Notwithstanding this, few American bankers realised that President Roosevelt was fighting their battle. The United States is by no means the only country where it would be to the interest of bankers to raise commodity prices by means of moderate inflation. A substantial rise in world prices would unfreeze a very large proportion of frozen indebtedness. It would enable bankers to bring Standstill Agreements to an end and to write up assets which had been treated as bad or doubtful. Indeed, unless such a rise in commodity prices takes place, most banks all over the world will remain for many years under the handicap of losses inherited from the crisis. The banking history of the next decade or two will be characterised by a long series of reconstructions, and the enterprising spirit of the banks will remain perpetually damped by the necessity of nursing weak positions.

### (3) OPPOSITION TO REFLATION

In the circumstances, it is difficult to understand the stubborn opposition of most bankers to a policy of reflation, however moderate it may be. Possibly it is due to fears that the Governments may not be able to check inflation before it goes too far. It is a habit of the opponents of inflation to utter solemn warnings against every departure from the canons of orthodox finance on the ground that, as a result, sterling will eventually share the fate of the German mark. Such arguments may go down with the audiences of Hyde Park orators, but we are entitled to expect bankers to realise how absurd they are. In order that sterling should share the fate of the mark, this country would have to lose a prolonged war, undergo a revolution and a military occupation of its industrial districts, and would have to be landed with reparations far in excess of its capacity to pay. Even then it is conceivable that the reaction of the British public and the British authorities to such a series of misfortunes might be different from that which was experienced in Germany in 1923.

In any case, unless and until such an utterly unlikely situation arises in this country, there is no need to fear extreme inflation. Bankers must be well aware of this, or certainly should be. If it is difficult to understand the opposition of bankers to reflation, their attitude towards credit expansion of a non-inflationary character is even more unintelligible. Given the fact that interest rates are low and are likely to remain fairly low for some years to come, it is evidently in the interest of bankers to spread their heavy expenses over a larger volume of business. If the margin of interest rates is narrow, the remedy lies in an increase of turnover by means of an expansion of credit for productive purposes. For the present, the problem does not arise, since the demand for credit is relatively moderate. Should trade continue to expand, however, bankers will soon be confronted with the dilemma of whether or not it is safe to extend credit further. Public opinion, in Great Britain at any rate, is becoming increasingly pressing in favour of a more liberal credit policy, and if they should revert to their pre-crisis attitude, banks may further increase their unpopularity. It is to their interest, therefore, to adopt a less rigid attitude.

## (4) BANKS' LIMITED SCOPE

This does not, however, mean that under the cloak of a more liberal credit policy they should allow themselves to be bullied into granting risky credits. The first duty of the banker is towards his depositor, and credit expansion should never take place as a result of slackening the scrutiny with which applications are viewed. Before the crisis banks had to decline many applications, not because they did not consider the borrower reliable, but because it was contrary to their policy to go beyond a certain limit. In this direction there is a wide scope for credit expansion without involving any deterioration in the quality of the credit.

It is not the banks' business to finance speculative enterprise or to grant long-term financial facilities. In this latter respect, the agitation against the banks is particularly ill-advised. Doubtless it is desirable from the point of view of public interest that long-term facilities should be made available to a larger extent than they are at present. They are, however, outside the scope of the ordinary commercial bank. They should be provided by financial houses specialising in that kind of business, or they should, if necessary, be raised under Government guarantee. There is ample scope for commercial banks to expand their credit facilities without having to depart from their normal sphere of activity.

### (5) PLANNING AND CREDIT EXPANSION

The community is entitled to expect the banks to adopt a less timid policy towards credit expansion for productive purposes. At the same time, the banks are entitled to expect the community to provide the necessary guarantee that credit expansion will not lead to abuses in the form of over-speculation. As things are, there is not the slightest guarantee that an expansion of credit would not be diverted into wrong channels. Even though the banks would be careful to grant credit only for productive purposes, indirectly the surplus resources would become available for financing a speculative boom. In order that it should become safe for the bankers to assist production by an expansion of credit, it would be essential to take steps for the prevention of excessive speculation. New issues should be subject to closer scrutiny on the part of the Stock Exchange Committee, and there should be a closer collaboration between banks and the authorities to prevent over-production in certain branches.

This is not the place to discuss in detail the nature and extent of economic planning that would be required to prevent trade expansion from developing into a dangerous boom. Our point is that the attitude taken up by bankers towards expansionary proposals is mistaken. Instead of rigidly refusing to depart from orthodox principles, and thereby shouldering the whole unpopularity of their policy, they ought to insist upon coupling credit expansion with the safeguards of economic planning. In doing so, they would avoid appearing as the villains of the piece. They would counteract the development of the idea that bankers constitute the main obstacle to an increase in production and consumption and to an improvement in the standard of living. They would to a large extent disarm the demand for the nationalisation of the banks, which is gaining adherents to an increasing degree, largely owing to the rigid orthodoxy of bankers. It is to the interest of the bankers to dispel the impression that their attitude is one of uncompromising orthodoxy. It is to their interest to make the public realise that they are quite willing to do their share in any sensible scheme for expanding production, provided that they can do so without running undue risks. While bankers should continue to oppose excessive inflation, they should be able to discriminate between it and moderate inflation, between destructive and constructive inflation, and between uncontrolled and controlled inflation.

# FRANCE'S CRISIS

## (1) VARIOUS ASPECTS OF THE CRISIS

Is France's crisis over or is it yet to come? This question has been the subject of lively controversy in and outside France during the past eighteen months. Many people believe that the French crisis attained its climax with the political crisis of May 1935, and that ever since good progress has been made towards political, economic, and financial consolidation. This view, however, is regarded by many students of the French situation as being unduly optimistic. They regard such recovery as has taken place under the Government of National Union headed by M. Laval as merely a temporary phase that will be followed by a relapse into a crisis.

The question is important, since stability and prosperity in France are essential to the peace and welfare of Europe. To answer it, let us see how the French crisis developed, examining one by one the various manifestations of the crisis, or to follow French usage, the various crises that have been running concurrently in France. In English we talk only about political crises, economic crises, and financial crises. Even the term "financial crisis" is considered by many as superfluous, for a financial crisis is usually a manifestation of an economic crisis. The French, on the other hand, talk about a variety of crises: the *crise budgétaire*, the *crise de Trésorerie*, the *crise monétaire*, the *crise bancaire*, the *crise économique*, the *crise politique*, and, of

course, the *crise de confiance* and the *crise morale*.
Although they are all part of the same crisis, they
should be considered separately, but without losing
sight of how they are related to one another. Each
crisis is the cause as well as the effect of others, and
it would be difficult to enumerate them in order of
importance. Let us begin with the comparatively
simple.

### (2) THE BUDGETARY CRISIS

First, the budgetary crisis. This seems to be a chronic
malady in France. Apart from the period between 1926
and 1931, the French Budget has closed with a deficit
every year since 1914. The traditional reluctance of
French taxpayers to pay taxes had made it impossible
for the Government to meet any part of the expenses
of the war and of the reconstruction of devastated
areas out of current revenue. The public debt thus
increased to over 300,000 million francs. This burden
became one of the principal obstacles to balancing the
Budget even after the work of reconstruction was
practically completed. There was, in addition, a Parliamentary deadlock between 1924 and 1926. The budgetary situation was becoming desperate, when at the
eleventh hour a Government of National Union was
formed under M. Poincaré, whose energetic measures
averted a financial collapse.

The French people, confronted with extreme emergency and stirred to patriotism by M. Poincaré, sub-
mitted to sacrifices in the form of higher taxation
and cuts in public expenditure. These sacrifices, however, were not unbearable, thanks to the period of
economic prosperity that preceded them and that
continued for years afterward. This is important, for

the French taxpayers could afford to pay the increased taxes and trade could afford to stand the curtailed expenditure because of the stabilisation of the franc at a level where it tended to stimulate business.

The period of prosperity that followed stabilisation enabled M. Poincaré to accumulate a substantial liquid reserve for the Treasury and to reduce the public debt by some 33,000 million francs by the end of 1930. This state of affairs was too good to last. Within a few years adverse conditions, coupled with reckless financial methods, brought France back to a situation like that of 1926. The budgetary surplus disappeared and gave way to a large deficit. The Treasury surplus was used up. The public debt rose to its 1926 level. By 1931 the French Budget was in the throes of a new crisis. This was partly due to circumstances over which neither the French Government nor Parliament nor the people had any control. The world economic crisis inevitably affected France, causing a reduction in incomes, which in turn reacted upon the yield of taxation. No Government, however skilful, and no taxpayers, however patriotic, could have prevented this development.

But there were other causes of the trouble for which Government, Parliament, and the people were to blame. In the first place, the deliberate deflationary policy pursued by the French Government was largely responsible for starting and accelerating the fall in commodity prices. Since a fall in prices inevitably leads to a decline in private earnings and correspondingly in public revenue, all the efforts of successive Finance Ministers to meet the deficiency were doomed to fail. The conditions that enabled M. Poincaré to balance his Budgets no longer existed. France had ceased to be economically prosperous.

## (3) THE CLIMAXES OF 1934 AND 1935

The will to take drastic measures to balance the Budget was also absent. Although some of the Finance Ministers, especially M. Germain Martin, tried hard to eliminate the deficit, they could not overcome the resistance to unpopular measures in the Cabinet, in the Finance Committee, in Parliament, and in the country at large. Between 1932 and 1934 this problem brought down one Government after another. The inability of Parliament to cope with the Budget was largely responsible for the decline of its prestige; but for this question the political troubles early in 1934 would probably never have occurred, or, at any rate, would have been much less violent. The demonstrators in the streets of Paris in February 1934 had the moral backing of a very large section of the French people because the Government and the whole Parliamentary system were so utterly discredited, largely on account of the budgetary deadlock.

With the establishment of the Government of National Union, the budgetary crisis temporarily relaxed. M. Doumergue, playing on the Radical-Socialist party's fears of a General Election, succeeded in passing M. Germain Martin's fiscal reform measures, thereby improving the budgetary situation beyond all hopes. Drastic economies reduced the deficit by 4000 million francs. It was claimed at the time that through these measures the Budget was balanced, but subsequent revenue returns proved that the rejoicing was premature. As was to be expected, drastic reduction of expenditure aggravated the economic depression and brought about a considerable decline in revenue.

This state of affairs continued after M. Flandin suc-

ceeded M. Doumergue, and by the end of 1934 it had
to be admitted that the Budget for 1935 would close
with a huge deficit. In accordance with French fiscal
tradition, the Government did its utmost to disguise
this unpleasant fact. On paper the deficit was reduced
to a negligible figure, but various items were excluded.
Expenditure on national defence and on the Government's wheat and wine valorisation scheme was placed
outside the Budget. The railway deficit of some 4000
million francs, for which the Government was responsible, was also omitted. Taking everything into consideration, the total amount which the Treasury was
called upon to find for current requirements during
1935 was estimated at between 12,000 million and
14,000 million francs.

M. Flandin, in order to be able to tackle the budgetary problem, wanted to obtain full powers from Parliament to govern by decree for a limited period. He was,
however, defeated, and so was his immediate successor,
M. Buisson, whose Finance Minister, M. Caillaux,
claimed to have produced a scheme for putting the
Budget on a sound basis. They were succeeded by M.
Laval, who at last obtained from Parliament the
powers requested.

### (4) M. LAVAL'S ECONOMIES

On July 17, 1935, M. Laval published his first batch
of decrees, which contained unexpectedly drastic
measures for eliminating the deficit. Although the
book-keeping jugglery which has come to be regarded
as traditional in French Budgets was not altogether
absent, to a very large extent the deficit was reduced
by means of genuine economies and to a smaller extent

P

by means of new taxation. There was a 10 per cent all-round cut in every expenditure item with the exception of the expenditure on national defence. Much to the surprise of everybody, even interest on public debt was arbitrarily reduced by 10 per cent. As a result of these drastic measures, the budgetary deficit was, if not altogether eliminated, certainly reduced to within manageable proportions.

Notwithstanding this, it would be unduly optimistic to say that the French budgetary crisis is over. Indeed, there is every reason to believe that the worst is yet to come. The economic indices point to a considerable decline in trade during the second half of 1934, and during 1935. This is bound to react unfavourably upon revenue. Within twelve months of their application, M. Germain Martin's economies resulted in a corresponding decline in budgetary receipts. The effect of M. Laval's economies is likely to manifest itself even sooner, because in order to make the cuts in Civil Service wages more bearable he endeavoured to reduce the cost of living by decree. Rents, interest on mortgages, gas, electricity, coal, meat, etc., were reduced by about 10 per cent, and efforts were made to reduce also other items of the cost of living. As a result, taxable incomes and purchasing power will contract more rapidly than after M. Germain Martin's economies. Before very long, a huge deficit will inevitably reappear as a result of the fall in revenue.

Will M. Laval in an effort to balance the Budget of 1936 resort to a repetition of the drastic economy measures he enforced in July last? It is doubtful whether he will be either politically or economically in a position to do so. Further attempts to balance the Budget by means of economies must aggravate depression and thereby cause a fresh decline in revenue. Budgetary expenditure, trade depression, and budgetary revenue are moving in a vicious circle, and there is no hope of breaking it except through drastic reflationary measures that would improve trade and provide a much-needed relief to the Budget. Unless the strain on the Budget is relaxed by a reasonable devaluation of the franc, it will become a permanent obstacle to the return to a sound budgetary situation.

## (5) THE TREASURY'S CRISIS

A budgetary deficit in itself is no disaster. Under ordinary conditions the French Government, with its excellent record as a debtor, should find it easy to cover the deficit by borrowing in the normal way. The difficulty lies in the distrust of the French investor. On various occasions since the war the Treasury has been unable to raise in the capital market the funds it required. More than once, especially between 1924 and 1926, the Treasury's liquid reserve has fallen to a dangerously low level. On several occasions the Treasury's balance with the Bank of France was for some time under 100 million francs—barely sufficient to cover a few days' current requirements. M. Poincaré succeeded in accumulating a Treasury surplus of some 14,000 million, but his successors lost no time in spending it. In France it is said to be unsafe to show a Treasury surplus, since it encourages Parliament to be extravagant. M. Poincaré's surplus was, in fact, used up partly by current budgetary deficits and partly by the support the Tardieu and Laval Governments granted to various banks and foreign Governments that got into difficulties during the crisis.

From 1932 onwards, the position of the Treasury became once more precarious. While in other countries the depression drove a large part of the capital formerly used by industry and commerce into Government securities, in France the safety-first movement led to hoarding. The Treasury was unable to issue long-term loans except on highly onerous and humiliating terms, and the French money market provided no facilities for any substantial Treasury bill issues. Although the leading banks were ready to take over a certain amount, their absorbing capacity was limited by their having to maintain abnormally large liquid cash reserves. On three occasions, in 1933, 1934, and 1935, in order to meet the most urgent requirements the Treasury found it necessary to raise credits abroad.

The loan operations carried out as a result of the temporary improvement that came with the advent of the Government of National Union admittedly relieved the Treasury situation towards the end of 1934. At the beginning of 1935, the Treasury's balance with the Bank of France amounted to about 1000 million francs. But the fact that the Budget was hopelessly unbalanced continued to preoccupy the Treasury, and called for measures to secure its requirements of funds for the future. The Government decided, at the beginning of 1935, to make Treasury bills eligible for rediscount with the Bank of France. This attempt was, however, frustrated as a result of the passive resistance displayed by the regents and permanent officials of the Bank of France. A compromise was eventually reached by which the Central Bank was prepared to grant loans not exceeding thirty days upon the security of Treasury bills. Until the crisis of May 1935, the amount of such loans was negligible.

## (6) ATTITUDE OF BANK OF FRANCE

Indeed, it was the aim of the Bank of France to keep the Treasury on short rations so as to compel Government and Parliament to take the drastic deflationary measures required to balance the Budget. M. Flandin, who was an anti-deflationist, was unable to put his reflationary policy into operation, and in order to save the Treasury from ignominious insolvency he had to submit to the dictation of the financial interests behind the Bank of France.

During the acute crisis in May and June 1935, the Bank of France provided some assistance to meet the immediate requirements of the Treasury, but took good care not to be over-generous until Parliament had granted the Government the exceptional powers required for the passing of unpopular measures. Even after the publication of M. Laval's decrees, the Treasury's cash supplies were kept at a low ebb so as to keep the Treasury in a state of perpetual dependence upon the Bank of France.

While in 1934 the economy measures of M. Doumergue were followed by the issue of a number of loans which improved the Treasury's position, there have been hardly any new Government issues since M. Laval's economy measures. Indeed the arbitrary cut in the interest rate on Government debt by 10 per cent was not exactly helpful for new Government financing. If the cut has to be repeated in order to balance the Budget for 1936, the Treasury's chances of meeting its requirements by loans will further decline.

It is true that M. Laval has taken a leaf out of M. Flandin's book by adopting his policy of monetary reflation. While pursuing ruthless deflation through budgetary economies and price reductions, he has shown himself anxious to make money cheaper, and to that end has reverted to M. Flandin's scheme of rediscounting Treasury bills with the Bank of France. He hopes that in doing so the Treasury's task of placing new short-term loans will be facilitated and that eventually the wholesale dishoarding of funds will enable the Government to issue long-term loans. Amidst the prevailing distrust and uncertainty, it is difficult, however, to see how his hopes can materialise. Indeed there is every reason to believe that before many months the Treasury will once more be confronted with an acute crisis, which can only lead to inflationary borrowing from the Bank of France.

### (7) THE BANKING CRISIS

The Treasury's difficulties were, as we have seen, originally due in part to the necessity of supporting banks that were in trouble. The banking crisis in France was indeed of exceptional severity. It reached its climax with the difficulties of the Banque Nationale de Crédit in October 1931, which provoked a wholesale withdrawal of deposits from practically all banks. If the Treasury had not gone to the rescue of the Banque Nationale de Crédit, there would have been a general run on the banks, and a collapse would have been unavoidable. As it was, the banks succeeded in saving themselves, but only at the price of aggravating the economic crisis by ruthlessly calling in credits.

The banking crisis began to abate in 1932, and by 1933 it was entirely over. Fortunately, it reached its climax while the Treasury was still able to grant support. If the climax had come two years later, the

Government would have faced the dilemma of letting
the banks fail or declaring a general moratorium, or
else supporting them by means of inflationary borrowing from the Bank of France. But the banks weathered
the political and budgetary crises of 1933–1935 without much difficulty. The withdrawals of deposits during
the panics of February 1934 and May 1935 were not
sufficiently large to endanger their position, and after
the end of these crises the money previously withdrawn
gradually found its way back to the banks. Not only
did the banks not require help during that period, but
they themselves assisted the Treasury to no slight
extent by taking up Treasury bills within the limits of
their capacity.

There were no bank failures worth mentioning during
1934 and 1935; yet the prospects are far from reassuring. Although by the beginning of 1934 the banks
had eliminated their bad debts, in the course of the
past year the deepening of the economic crisis has
resulted in new bad debts. The difficulties of the
Societé Financière Speciale, the Citroën Company, and
other concerns at the end of 1934 inflicted heavy losses
upon the banks, and further losses are likely. Should
they grow to such an extent as to alarm the French
public, we may witness another run of depositors, and
this time the Treasury will not have available liquid
resources to support the banks. Moreover, a flight from
the franc assumes largely the form of withdrawals of
deposits for the purpose of transferring the funds
abroad or hoarding them in the form of gold. If both
the Treasury and the banks require assistance at the
same time, and they are unable to help each other,
then the Government would have to fall back upon
the Bank of France and inflation would be inevitable.

## (8) THE MONETARY CRISIS

This brings us to the French monetary crisis. Because of the measures taken by M. Poincaré, the post-war monetary crisis ended in 1926. The franc was stabilised. Thanks to the repatriation of French funds that took refuge abroad during the inflation, and to the favourable trade balance, brought about by the undervaluation of the currency, the Bank of France accumulated a huge gold and foreign exchange reserve. The technical position of the franc became very strong indeed. After the repatriation of practically the entire foreign exchange reserve during 1931 and 1932 the reserve ratio rose to about 80 per cent, which is twice the legal minimum. The French authorities defended the franc by applying a time-honoured orthodox device. They raised the bank rate whenever there was a persistent outflow of gold, even if in doing so they accentuated the business depression. The Government pursued a policy of cutting down expenditure and encouraged private employers to do likewise. It was hoped that this deflationary drive would place the franc above suspicion.

But the French public remained profoundly distrustful of the franc. The hoarding of gold assumed unprecedented proportions, and from time to time there was a flight from the national currency; for instance, towards the end of 1932 and in the early months of 1933, and again towards the turn of 1933. The French public was reluctant to trust the franc mainly because of the budgetary and the Treasury crises. Although the Bank of France refused to finance the deficit, it was evident that, if the Government should find no other means of raising the amount required, it would overcome the resistance of the bank and the deficit would be covered by inflationary borrowing. It was largely the anticipation of such developments that from time to time caused a flight from the franc. The flight from the franc assumed considerable proportions at the beginning of 1934, partly owing to the budgetary crisis but largely owing to the political crisis. Between April 1934 and April 1935 the Bank of France succeeded, however, in recovering the gold it lost during the last crisis. In May 1935 the flight from the franc was renewed and assumed unprecedented dimensions. The loss of gold attained record figures. At the same time, the Bank of France was unable to pursue its traditional orthodox policy of reducing its sight liabilities in proportion to the loss of gold. As a result of the Treasury's requirements and also of the withdrawals of deposits from banks, the Central Bank had to expand credit instead of restricting it.

With the advent of M. Laval's Government the panic subsided, but in spite of the drastic economy measures confidence was not restored to a sufficient degree to bring about a wholesale repatriation and dishoarding of funds. During June the Bank of France continued to lose gold, and the amount recovered during July and August was relatively small. Evidently the example of Belgium, which country had to abandon the defence of its currency under the weight of irresistible pressure, had a demoralising effect upon the French public. In any case, the uncertainty of the internal and international political outlook inspired distrust in the stability of the franc. While the outflow of capital was more or less checked, there was no sign of a reversal of the movement on any scale comparable with the reversal that followed the crisis of February 1934.

## (9) THE ECONOMIC CRISIS

Another reason why the French public fears a depreciation of the franc is because of the adverse effect it would have on trade. Owing to the low rate of stabilisation chosen by M. Poincaré the franc was grossly undervalued until the end of 1931. Then it became heavily overvalued in comparison with the depreciated currencies. Despite all the inflationary efforts, equilibrium could not be restored between French commodity prices and world prices. Consequently it was difficult for France to export and she had to resort to various kinds of measures to reduce her imports—measures that tended to maintain high prices and led to reprisals by foreign countries against French exports. Invisible exports such as the money spent by foreign tourists and the yield of foreign investments also declined considerably. M. Laval's declared intention is to remove the quotas on imports in order to reduce prices. Should he do so, however, a series of adverse trade balances would undermine the technical strength of the franc. While export trade alone is not of sufficient importance to France, the growing depression in home trade tends to encourage a strong movement in favour of devaluation. Indeed, the number of the supporters of M. Paul Reynaud, who is in favour of a devaluation of the franc, is increasing daily. The discontent caused by M. Laval's measures also tends to augment the camp of devaluationists. It appears, indeed, that the crisis of the franc is by no means over.

The economic crisis was almost entirely unknown in France until the end of 1931. The post-war slump of 1920–1921 was followed by a rapid recovery as a result of inflationary spending by the Government, while owing to the undervaluation of the franc France escaped the stabilisation crisis that affected many other countries. After 1929, when the depression became world-wide, France appeared to be immune. This was due partly to her comparative self-sufficiency and partly to the undervaluation of the franc. It was not until Great Britain went off gold that France began to feel the economic crisis. During the following three years the depression increased gradually. The difficulties of the Citroën Company at the end of 1934 provided some indication of the effects on trade of deflation and of overvaluing the franc. There is no reason whatsoever to believe that in this respect the worst is over. Even if the French Government should cease to deflate any further, the deflationary drive of 1935 has yet to produce its full effect upon trade.

Admittedly, the new French Government adopted the policy of assisting trade by making money cheaper. It is as yet doubtful whether this object will be achieved. In any case, the extent to which trade recovery can be brought about by means of cheap money alone is negligible. Thus the chances are that the French economic crisis will continue. This must accentuate the budgetary crisis, the Treasury crisis, and the banking crisis, and through its psychological effect it may lead to a renewed monetary crisis. Owing to the demoralising effect of prolonged depression, it may also become a cause of a renewed political crisis.

## (10) PSYCHOLOGICAL FACTORS

The actual figures of the French financial and economic situation are in themselves by no means alarming. It is through the exaggeration of their effect on the *crise de confiance* and the *crise morale* that they may produce disastrous consequences. The *crise de confiance*, or wave of distrust, has been the direct cause of most of France's troubles since the war. The chaotic conditions between 1923 and 1926 arose largely from the distrust that accentuated to the extreme all the adverse material factors. M. Poincaré's drastic measures restored confidence in 1926, and it was not until 1931 that France again relapsed into a *crise de confiance*. This time it took the form of a banking crisis, and, during the subsequent years, of repeated flights from the franc. M. Doumergue's advent restored confidence once more. But as the flight from the franc during the political troubles of October and November 1934 indicated, the basis of this newly acquired confidence was none too solid. It disappeared once more in May 1935. As we pointed out above, confidence failed to return after the solution of the political crisis in June 1935. While the acute panic ceased the atmosphere remained strained. Any adverse development in the economic, financial, or political sphere would be capable of provoking a fresh *crise de confiance*.

As to the *crise morale*, recent financial scandals indicate that it is still acute. It began in 1930, even before the beginning of the economic and financial crises. Highly placed politicians were involved in a series of financial scandals. The most notorious were the Oustric affair, the case of Mme Hanau, and, over and above all, the Stavisky case. The last named

wrecked two Governments, and was largely responsible
for the street riots in February 1934. It disclosed a
hitherto unsuspected degree of corruption among
politicians, in Government Departments, and even in
the administration of justice. Confidence in the whole
Parliamentary democratic system of the Third Republic appeared to be shaken to its very foundations.

This was only one manifestation of the *crise morale*.
The exaggeration of the significance of financial
scandals led to a state of demoralisation the extent of
which few people outside France realised. The Stavisky
disclosures led the public to suspect scandals every-
where. It was whispered that the fortifications on the
eastern frontier on which many milliards of francs had
been spent were worthless, as a large part of the money
remained in the hands of intermediaries. It was said
that the machines of the air force were hopelessly
obsolete, and that corruption connected with army
contracts had reduced the value of French defensive
forces to insignificance. Indeed there were wholesale
desertions from the French Army, and the Government, for fear of publicity, did not dare to prosecute
deserters.

The political truce and the improved budgetary
situation under M. Doumergue halted the *crise morale*.
But no wholesale purging of political life took place,
for that would have ended the political truce. The
Stavisky enquiry was dragging on month after month
without result. New scandals were discovered towards
the end of 1934, and the year closed under the shadow
of the Citroën affair. The year 1935, too, had its crop
of financial scandals, though nothing comparable to
the Stavisky affair. It would be unduly optimistic to
suppose that the *crise morale* in France has come to an

end. Even if at present there are no signs of such demoralisation as was witnessed in 1934, prospects of a national regeneration, which alone can put an end to the *crise morale,* are completely lacking.

## (11) THE POLITICAL CRISIS

Given the financial, economic, and psychological crises France experienced during the last four years, and given her peculiar Parliamentary system, the country had inevitably to go through a series of political crises. Ever since 1932 changes of Government have been frequent and some Ministries have lasted only a few weeks; one of them, in fact, lasted only a few days. Political instability and the absence of a dependable majority for any Government have aggravated the crisis in all its manifestations. The financial recovery of 1934 was largely the result of the comparative political stability brought about by the formation of the Doumergue Government. The political truce continued when M. Flandin became Premier.

While M. Doumergue sought to cure the evil of frequent political crises by changing the Constitution, M. Flandin abandoned the idea and concentrated upon removing the causes of discontent through an improvement in the economic situation. Partly for this reason he decided to discard the orthodox deflationary policy of his predecessors and to devise measures that in given circumstances might result in reflation. The failure of his attempt and his decision to revert to the deflationary monetary policy dictated by the Bank of France led to the political crisis of May 1935. After his defeat and that of M. Buisson, it appeared as though it was impossible to form a Government with a working majority. The Radical-Socialist party, however, intimidated by signs of renewed unrest in the street, gave its support to M. Laval, who received authority to govern until November 1935 by means of decree. Parliament was dissolved and for five months at any rate France was to enjoy internal political stability.

Notwithstanding this, and in spite of the fact that M. Laval's drastic measures met with relatively little violent opposition, the political outlook remains obscure. It is generally assumed that when Parliament reassembles in November, and when it becomes evident that new sacrifices will be required to balance the Budget for 1936, fresh political troubles will arise. There is, it is true, some talk about the possibility of a compromise by which M. Laval should summon the National Assembly in order to postpone the General Election due in the spring of 1936. In return for this, the deputies would renew every six months the exceptional powers conferred upon him. Even if M. Laval were successful in carrying out this scheme, it would not save him from internal political troubles. Indeed there is reason to fear that since the discontent of the nation with the Government's policy would be prevented from expressing itself through constitutional channels, it would seek unconstitutional channels. The Socialists and Communists, who at present want to avoid violence owing to the proximity of the General Election when they hope to obtain a majority, are likely to resort to unconstitutional means if the election is postponed. Indeed there is some reason to fear that the *crise politique* in France may develop into a *crise de régime*.

In the sphere of international politics there were some signs of improvement early in 1935 owing to the *rapprochement* with Italy and with Soviet Russia. As a result of the Abyssinian conflict, however, which opens up the possibility of grave repercussions in Europe and a complete regrouping of powers, the international outlook has also become gloomy. An international rearmament race is now a certainty, and this, together with periodical war scares, will constitute an additional disturbing factor in the French situation.

### (12) CONCLUSION

Thus in several spheres the French crisis is still going on unabated, even though in some spheres it is of a chronic rather than acute nature. The Budget is still unbalanced; the Treasury position remains weak; the economic situation is changing from bad to worse; the *crise morale* continues, even though in a less spectacular fashion. In other directions the crisis has abated, but all the elements for its renewal are present.

What, then, is the way out of the crisis? The answer is: Through the devaluation of the franc. In abandoning the stubborn struggle to maintain the franc at its parity, the French Government would remove one of the main causes of the crisis. A reasonable devaluation would enable the Government to balance the Budget and thus also remove the cause of the Treasury crisis. The franc, at a lower level, would enjoy confidence; funds would return from their hiding-places; trade would revive; the disaster of a banking crisis would no longer threaten; the *crise de confiance* would come to an end; all this improvement would prepare the way for the elimination of the *crise morale*, and would make for a reasonable political stability. Even in international relations the devaluation of the franc would strengthen France, since it would enable her to spend, if necessary, huge amounts for her national defence.

It would be a mistake to say that devaluation would solve the entire problem. What is wanted is a thorough national regeneration, which cannot, however, be achieved unless the franc is devalued. Confronted with the menace of Hitler's Germany, France cannot afford to waste her energies in bolstering up the franc at an untenable level. In any case, she is heavily handicapped in the coming fight for her existence. The French nation is not mechanically minded in an age of increasing mechanisation. It is not efficient in an age in which efficient organisation is ever increasingly important. It clings to its nineteenth-century system of *laissez-faire* while other nations make more or less rapid progress towards economic planning.

Over and above these and many other disadvantages, it would be suicidal for France to go on handicapping herself deliberately by maintaining the franc at an overvalued level. It is to her interest to concentrate all her available energies upon working out her salvation by a fundamental regeneration instead of upon the defence of the present unnatural parities of the franc. The French nation has to realise before it is too late that the choice lies between the franc and France.

# GERMANY'S ECONOMIC RECOVERY

## (1) POLITICS AND ECONOMICS

EVER since the advent of the Hitler régime, the attention of the world has become focussed upon Germany. The situation and prospects of that country provide an inexhaustible topic of discussion and ample material for controversy. Is the régime likely to last? What will be the outcome of the struggle between its Conservative and Radical supporters? Will Germany's foreign policy lead to another European war? These are the questions which are the subject of heated discussions day after day whenever people interested in international affairs meet. They are essentially political questions, but they cannot be answered adequately without a thorough knowledge of the economic background.

National Socialism in Germany stands or falls with the success or failure of the efforts to improve economic conditions. Herr Hitler came into power as a result of the deflationary crisis, and in the long run he can only remain the ruler of Germany if he can bring about a recovery. The answer to the question whether in domestic politics Germany will move to the Left or to the Right also depends to a large degree upon economic considerations. The balance of power between industrialists and bankers and other Conservative elements on the one hand and the extremists of the National Socialist party on the other will be decided largely by the economic factor.

Even the question of war and peace is to some extent connected with the economic evolution of National Socialist Germany.

The economic aspects of National Socialism are as highly controversial as its political aspects. Has there been an economic recovery in Germany since 1933, and, if so, what were its main causes? To what extent has Germany departed from *laissez-faire* capitalism? Is Germany heading towards an economic collapse? What will be the fate of Germany's debts, domestic and foreign? These and many other questions call for an answer if one is to form a judgment about the prospects of the new régime in Germany.

## (2) RECOVERY SINCE 1933

There can be no doubt that economic recovery in Germany since the beginning of 1933 has been greater than in any other country. According to official statistics, the number of unemployed has declined from about six millions to well under two. Even though official figures from present-day Germany should be taken with a grain of salt, there can be no doubt that the extent of the trade revival has been spectacular. There is every evidence of increased industrial activity; in addition to the employment which has been provided by public works and rearmament, the revival of trade has also been stimulated by a genuine increase of demand by consumers. The banks have succeeded in liquidating by far the greater part of the frozen credits inherited from the crisis of 1931. The Government's expenditure on unemployment benefits has declined sharply, while taxation revenue has increased.

To some extent the improvement has been due to
the world-wide recovery initiated by the suspension
of the gold standard in the United States. All countries
over the five continents shared in this recovery with
the exception of those which insisted upon continuing a self-torturing deflationary policy. Germany was
not amongst them and took her share in the benefit
from the upward turn in the world trend. This in
itself accounts, however, for only a fraction of the
improvement witnessed in Germany. For the most
part, this improvement has been due to the unscrupulous and unorthodox economic and financial policy
pursued by the Hitler régime.

The economic policy of National Socialism has been
unscrupulous because it has brought about economic
recovery at the expense of Germany's foreign creditors.
It was unorthodox because to a high degree it violated
the principles of *laissez-faire* and those of "sound"
finance. Indeed it may be said that, apart from Soviet
Russia, there is no other country in which *laissez-faire*
has been discarded to such an extent as in Germany.
Although Italy served as a model for the German
economic policy, the pupil in this case, as in so many
other cases, surpassed his master.

### (3) PUBLIC WORKS AND REARMAMENT

Public-works schemes and rearmament on a large
scale were to a great extent responsible for the economic recovery. In the absence of reliable figures, it
is impossible to make a comparison between the
extraordinary expenditure of this kind in Germany
and in the United States. It ought to be borne in
mind, however, that Germany launched out her

ambitious public-works schemes when her gold reserve was practically exhausted and when the financial resources of her investors, already depleted by the inflation of 1923, had been heavily reduced by the crisis of 1931. The United States and other countries which embarked upon ambitious public-works schemes have been spending what they have possessed. Germany, on the other hand, has embarked upon spending non-existent milliards. This fact in itself would justify placing Germany in the front rank of capitalist countries pursuing an unorthodox policy.

The National Socialist régime, however, went much further in its pursuit of a highly unorthodox economic policy. Employment was created not merely by means of public works and rearmament but also by much more artificial means. During 1933, industrial employers were called upon to re-engage a certain number of workmen. Whether or not they were in a position to keep the additional workmen occupied, they had to put them on their wages lists. Protests and complaints were of no avail. To encourage such artificial re-employment, manufacturers were ordered to replace their machinery by less efficient machinery requiring the employment of a larger number of workmen. Such a degree of interference with private business is entirely without precedent in a modern capitalist State. To find a precedent we have to go back to the guild system of the Middle Ages.

Most people were convinced that such an additional burden on industrial undertakings would prove ruinous. In reality, it accentuated trade revival to no slight degree, for the additional wages paid out to the workmen created additional purchasing power. If only one employer had been compelled to engage a thousand workmen he did not want he would doubtless have been ruined, for he would have had to stand the full burden of the wages of a thousand unnecessary hands, while the extent to which he would have benefited by their additional purchasing power would have been infinitesimal. As, however, a very large number of employers were compelled to employ additional labour, they ended by obtaining a fair share in the total increase of purchasing power.

The revival of employment, which at the beginning was highly artificial, ended by becoming natural, and by 1934 there was no longer any need to resort to such arbitrary measures in order to reduce unemployment. Manufacturers were allowed to discard the less efficient machinery they had been compelled to introduce and were no longer called upon to employ workmen they did not want.

## (4) FINANCING OF RECOVERY

In the meantime the milliards spent on public works and rearmament went round and round in the vicious circle of trade. They enabled manufacturers and merchants to repay their frozen credits to their banks. The latter were able to redeem their frozen bills from the Reichsbank and other institutions created for the purpose of carrying the crisis bills. Both Government banks and commercial banks were thus placed in a position to finance public works. Treasury bills had gradually taken the place of frozen commercial bills. The financing of public works and rearmament went on therefore without a hitch. There was no need to resort to crude measures of currency inflation in order to cover the huge deficit of the Reich.

In his recent Königsberg speech, Dr. Schacht, President of the Reichsbank and Minister of National Economy, stated that the reason why Germany was able to finance her public works was that she was an authoritative State and that under a Parliamentary system it would have been impossible to carry out that task. There is much truth in this remark. The budgetary deficit in Germany is probably much larger than that of France. In spite of this, nothing is said about it in the German Press or in public speeches. In France whenever Parliament discusses the budgetary deficit there is bound to be a Cabinet crisis and a financial panic. In Germany the problem of the deficit is simply not discussed in public. This does not, of course, mean that the problem does not exist. After all, even dictators are subject to the inexorable rules of simple arithmetic. Notwithstanding this, the budgetary deficit which from time to time has led to a Treasury crisis in France has not so far produced such an effect in Germany. If the German Treasury requires additional funds, the resources of banks, savings banks, and insurance companies, etc., are commandeered for the use of the Treasury. This is what happened in January 1935 when the savings banks were called upon to take over a loan of 500 million reichsmarks. Subsequently the insurance companies were ordered to take over a similar amount. Admittedly, the resources of these institutions are by no means inexhaustible. As, however, the money that is borrowed is spent immediately, in the ordinary course it returns to the source from which it was borrowed. This is what actually happened in the case of the savings banks, whose deposits have increased since the beginning of the year by rather more than the 500 million reichsmarks borrowed by the Government. In fact, in August, the Treasury was in a position to repeat the operation and ordered the savings banks to take over another 500 million reichsmarks.

## (5) PROPHECIES OF "COLLAPSE"

As a result of the unorthodox policy adopted, a trade revival was initiated which apparently continues to feed itself. The question is, Can it go on indefinitely? Is there no likelihood of a break in this vicious circle? The whole improvement appears to be utterly unnatural to those brought up on the teachings of conventional nineteenth-century economics. This is the reason why, ever since the first sign of improvement became noticeable, there has been no lack of gloomy prophecies outside Germany as to the inevitability of a collapse. Few of the prophets took the trouble to define exactly what they meant by "collapse". If all they meant was that Germany would default on her foreign debt, events have amply justified their forecast. Default on foreign debts, deplorable as it is from the point of view of creditors, is not, however, in itself a collapse. If the prophets meant by collapse a depreciation of the reichsmark, events have not quite justified their pessimism. The reichsmark is still at its old parity, and from time to time it appreciates to such an extent as to cause an influx of gold from France and Holland. It is true that there are various kinds of blocked marks—registered marks, credit marks, security marks, etc.—which are at a heavy discount, but from the point of view of the predominant majority of the German public, the rate at which these blocked marks are quoted is of no great importance. If the pessimistic prophets forecasting the doom of Germany meant an internal collapse, they were utterly wrong, for, much as we may dislike admitting it, economic conditions under the Hitler régime have improved considerably. Minor relapses and seasonal fluctuations apart, the trend of trade in Germany has been consistently on the up-grade since the first quarter of 1933.

The degree of improvement has surpassed even the anticipations of the supporters of the National Socialist régime. Some of them, brought up in the old school, viewed the unorthodox economic policy with profound distrust. Dr. Schacht himself, among others, was decidedly against the lavish expenditure on public works and rearmament. The story goes that when his protest against unsound finance was of no avail he threatened to resign, whereupon Herr Hitler told him that the alternative to the presidency of the Reichsbank was the concentration camp. Thereupon Dr. Schacht had to undertake the execution of a policy of which he disapproved. It must be admitted, however, that he carried out his task with absolute loyalty and with remarkable efficiency.

It is a curious coincidence that both in Germany and in Italy—where Signor Beneduce holds the key position for the execution of Fascist economic policy —the economic affairs of the régime are in the hands of experts who do not believe in the policy which they have to put into operation, and who nevertheless have made a success of their task.

## (6) BOOM AND TRADE BALANCE

It was not without reason that Dr. Schacht and other orthodox experts were doubtful about the success of the National Socialist economic policy. There was a danger that it might collapse as a result of the international repercussions of the internal recovery. Indeed, those in responsible positions in Germany had some very anxious months towards the end of 1934. It is only natural that the internal boomlet should tend to raise inland prices; this again had unfavourable repercussions upon Germany's capacity to export. At the same time, raw material imports had to be increased owing to the larger requirements of home industries. The result was an unfavourable change in the German trade balance. The surplus gave way to a deficit. Owing to this Germany ceased to pay her foreign debts. Her foreign creditors were thus ruthlessly sacrificed for the sake of the internal recovery. The result of Germany's default, however, was that German importers were no longer able to buy goods on a credit basis. It became increasingly difficult during the second half of 1934 to buy the raw materials required by German industries. Fears of a shortage of raw materials led to hasty purchases of goods of every kind by consumers, and this, while stimulating the trade revival, accentuated the rising tendency of the price-level. Owing to the unfavourable repercussions of this development upon German exports, there was a danger that the recovery might come to an abrupt end as a result of a raw material shortage. In fact, a number of factories had to reduce their activities owing to the inadequate supply of raw materials. This would have led to a relapse, but the Government intervened once more, forbidding the industrialists to dismiss any workmen on the ground of raw material shortage. Once more the employers protested in vain. They were assured, however, that they would obtain the raw materials required.

The German authorities took indeed drastic measures to that end. The whole import trade was brought under the Government's control so as to prevent the waste of foreign exchange resources upon unnecessary imports. The Government endeavoured to place Germany's trade relations with foreign countries on the basis of exchange clearing and compensation agreements. The application of that system made foreign countries realise that, in order to be able to sell to Germany and be paid for their exports, they had to import German goods. It was not easy to operate the system for German goods were too expensive. Dr. Schacht succeeded, however, in tiding his country over the critical period.

In order to facilitate the task of covering the country's raw material requirements, the Government resorted to additional drastic interference with private business. On Dr. Schacht's initiative, a special levy was raised from home industries for the purpose of subsidising export trade. The argument was that unless home industries which benefited by the internal boom were prepared to assist export trade, the latter would not be in a position to export a sufficient amount of goods to pay for the raw material imports indispensable for maintaining the internal recovery. This special levy was as unpopular among industrialists as were the earlier measures compelling them to employ unnecessary hands. They had to put up with

it, however, and while at the time of writing it is
premature to express an opinion about the results of
the new arrangement, there appears to be reason to
believe that the danger of a raw material shortage
has been overcome. While Germany cannot export
enough to pay her foreign debts, by hook or by crook
she is exporting enough to meet her raw material
requirements. There appears to be no immediate
danger from that side.

## (7) THE CONFIDENCE FACTOR

In his Königsberg speech, Dr. Schacht drew attention, however, to another source of danger. He pointed
out that the financing of extraordinary Government
expenditure can only go on so long as the public has
confidence in the financial stability of the country.
If, for some reason, the money spent by the Government fails to return to the banks, the latter will be
unable to lend it once more to the Treasury. In that
case, the Government will be confronted with the
dilemma of either financing its public works and rearmament by crude currency inflation or of reducing
the amount spent for these purposes. In either case
trouble would inevitably arise. There is, however, no
likelihood of the development of a wave of distrust.
While in France political instability is the main cause
of the periodical *crises de confiance*, Germany is
politically stable, and amidst the enthusiasm that
accompanies the regeneration of the German nation
there is no likelihood of any wave of distrust. In
any case, owing to existence of censorship—even Dr.
Schacht's speech was released for the German Press
only in an abridged form—criticism that might cause

uneasiness is non-existent in Germany. As for the
creation of panic through "whispering campaigns",
the German secret police is so well organised that
the danger is negligible.

According to Dr. Schacht, the main argument
against the devaluation of the reichsmark is that it
would undermine confidence and would therefore
wreck the Government's economic policy. In reality,
experience has proved over and over again that
devaluation or depreciation of a currency, far from
causing a panic, is the best way to bring a panic to
an end. This was the experience of Great Britain,
Japan, the Union of South Africa, the United States,
and quite recently of Belgium. There is no reason to
suppose it would be otherwise in Germany. On the
contrary, it is the prolonged resistance to devaluation
that might undermine confidence in financial stability
in Germany. It has been noticed that whenever there
is a flight from the gold currencies there is also an
internal flight from the reichsmark, on the assumption
that if the franc were devalued the reichsmark would
follow its example. The series of crises that are likely
to occur in the Gold Bloc may produce, therefore, unfavourable repercussions upon the German situation.
This is in fact the only danger spot that might conceivably reverse the trend of recovery.

## (8) INCREASING STATE CONTROL

There can be no doubt that the trend of evolution
in Germany points towards an increasing degree of
State control. While the régime does not aim at State
ownership of the means of production, it believes in
intervention to regulate business activity in accord-

ance with public interest. We have seen that in the course of the last three years the Government did not hesitate to compel private enterprise to take certain actions or abstain from taking certain actions. The object aimed at was that production and trade should regulate themselves with the aid of corporations and that the State should confine itself to the rôle of supreme arbitrator. The full development of the Corporate State is, however, in the distant and uncertain future, and in the meanwhile the Government intervenes directly.

The improvement of trade has strengthened the position of industrial interests. Notwithstanding this they are as far as ever from controlling the National Socialist State. As in Italy, so in Germany, the movement which was originally financed by industrialists as a means of fighting Communism and Socialism did not remain under their control. Indeed, some leading industrialists complain that they are little more than paid managers in their own enterprise. Should the extremist elements in the National Socialist party gain the upper hand, the fate of industrialists would not be much better than under a Communist régime and a good deal worse than it was under the Socialist Republic.

The chances are, however, that the balance of power in Germany will be held by the military caste during the coming year. The Reichswehr would not tolerate any development which under the cloak of radical National Socialism would virtually amount to Communism. On the other hand, the military caste is not likely to become the tool of the industrialists. In pre-war Germany the object of militarism was to serve the interests of industrial expansion. In present-day Germany, on the other hand, the object of industrial development will be to serve the interest of the military super-State that is being created. One of the reasons why discipline in the economic sphere has produced such satisfactory results in Germany is that the Germans are essentially a disciplined nation. All that is happening is that Prussian drill, instead of being confined to the barrack square, is now being applied to the economic system.

Whether or not the economic recovery continues, State interference has come to stay. While in countries with Parliamentary Democracy interventionism is considered purely temporary and is tolerated only because of the abnormal conditions, in National Socialist Germany it constitutes the fundamental principle of the official policy. The only difference a substantial economic improvement would make is that it would rule out the possibility of the balance of power shifting towards the Left. The business world would have to submit to dictation, but it would come from Conservative and not Radical quarters.

Opinions are divided as to the influence of Germany's economic recovery upon the prospects of peace. According to one opinion, the more conditions in Germany improve, the more she is able to accelerate her rearmament, the nearer the day is when she will consider herself strong enough to realise her ambitions. According to another opinion, the improvement of economic conditions in Germany and the Government's ability to cover raw material requirements reduces the chances of another war, for a prosperous nation is not likely to want to risk her existence in an adventure the outcome of which would be highly uncertain. Unfortunately, the first argument appears to be more convincing. Prosperity in 1914 did not prevent Germany from taking the risk of plunging the world into a war. From the point of view of world peace there is every reason, therefore, to view the spectacular recovery of Germany with concern.

# THE WAY OUT

## (1) AUTHOR'S APOLOGY

THE author fully realises that it is an unforgivable offence to add another to the innumerable proposals of the ways in which the depression could be brought to an end with a stroke of the pen. Since, however, he has abstained throughout the crisis from producing a "patent remedy" of his own, he feels he is entitled to claim lenient treatment under the First Offenders' Act. To reassure the reader, the author hastens to point out that he has no intention of proposing any monetary conjurer's tricks with the aid of which so many experts and pseudo-experts have claimed they could achieve the millennium. His proposal does not involve an inflationary increase in the monetary circulation or the establishment of a new kind of currency. Its other mitigating circumstances are that it does not presuppose a miraculous restoration of confidence, nor the successful conclusion of an international economic conference or any other form of altruistic international co-operation, nor any such Utopian dreams as render most world reconstruction schemes impracticable. Nor does it obviate the necessity for a drastic devaluation of all currencies, which in the author's view is the only method of eliminating the various disequilibria that would otherwise prevent the return of true prosperity. The proposed scheme would in a way complete the beneficial effect of a thoroughgoing devaluation.

R

Not the least of the advantages of the scheme is that it would be sufficient if the British Government were to agree to its adoption, since the rôle played by other Governments or other interests in its execution would be secondary. Nor would it cost a penny to the British taxpayer. Those who would derive direct benefit by it include raw material producers all over the world, debtors willing but unable to pay, and long-suffering creditors, British and foreign. It is impossible to think of anyone who would not benefit by it indirectly.

The proposal in question would bring the end of the depression nearer by reducing the surplus stocks of staple commodities and by raising their price; by reducing the volume of frozen debts affected by international transfer difficulties; by bringing nearer the moment when Great Britain would be in a position to stabilise sterling without taking undue risks. From a purely British point of view, the proposed scheme has the additional advantage of reducing the dependence of this country on foreign supplies of staple products; of placing in the hands of the British Government a powerful bargaining counter in international trade negotiations; and of facilitating the task of the British monetary authorities in maintaining the stability of sterling against adverse pressure without having to resort to a high bank rate.

## (2) A RAW MATERIAL RESERVE

Having aroused the curiosity of the reader with the aid of these preliminaries, we may now proceed to describe the scheme. Its substance is that the British Government should use the surplus it may obtain through the eventual revaluation of the gold held by the Bank of England and the Exchange Equalisation Account for the purpose of acquiring and holding reserve supplies in staple products. It should acquire these supplies from the debtor nations which are at present prevented by transfer difficulties from meeting their liabilities but which would be only too willing to pay provided that payment was accepted in the form of goods.

The scheme would work in the following way: The amounts that have accumulated in the various blocked accounts in raw-material-producing debtor countries would be used to purchase raw materials which would be taken over by the British Government. In order to satisfy the Governments of the debtor countries that the transaction would not reduce their chances of exporting their products against cash, the British Government would give the assurance that the commodities in question would be blocked for a period of at least two years. The equivalent of the purchase price of the commodities would be paid over to the British creditors by the British Government. Where the defaulting debtor was a foreign Government itself, it would have to issue internal bonds to the equivalent of the amount defaulted upon and spend the proceeds on the purchase of staple commodities which would be taken over by the British Government; the latter would then be able to pay the amount due to the British bondholders.

The list of commodities would include wheat, metals, cotton, wool, rubber, oil, etc. Their total amount should be determined by the net profit of the British Exchequer upon the revaluation of the gold reserves. It is reasonable to assume that, on the basis

of the present value of the pound, this net profit
would be at least £100 million. If the definite rate of
stabilisation of sterling is fixed below the present
level, then the amount in question will increase accordingly. Let us, however, for the sake of argument,
regard £100 million as the total of the operations. It
is perhaps a small amount compared with the total
value of surplus stocks in staple commodities. Nevertheless, if goods to a total of £100 million were lifted
out of the market, the reduction of supplies would
inevitably produce a rising tendency in prices. The
producers of the debtor countries would derive a
substantial direct benefit from the scheme, but the
rise in the world prices of commodities would be
beneficial to producers and holders of stocks all over
the world. Thus, producers in the British Dominions
would not be victimised by the transaction, even
though the purchases were made from foreign countries. The contraction of the surplus supplies would
be beneficial to all.

### (3) UNFREEZING BLOCKED ACCOUNTS

If £100 million is a small item compared with the
total of surplus staple commodities, it is a substantial
item compared with the total of blocked credits. While
the grand total of long, medium, and short-term debts
which is at present defaulted upon owing to transfer
difficulties must be many times larger, the actual
amounts on blocked accounts cannot greatly exceed
that figure. Their reduction by £100 million would
make an appreciable difference. The direct benefici-
aries would be those debtors who would thus recover
their solvency, and those creditors who would obtain

reimbursement. Indirectly, however, all debtors and
creditors would benefit, for the reduction of the
amount of frozen debts would improve the quality of
the outstanding balance. The significance of this consideration cannot be sufficiently estimated. It is a
commonplace of newspaper articles that there can
be no substantial revival in foreign trade without
the resumption of foreign lending. The reduction of
the total defaulted upon and the improvement of the
chances for the repayment or unfreezing of the rest
would go a very long way to prepare the ground for
the resumption of lending abroad.

This unfreezing of frozen credits is all the more
worth appreciating as in many cases the alternative
would be the loss of the whole or at least a great part
of the amounts involved. Barring a very sharp rise
in commodity prices, there is not the least chance
that the debt services of raw-material-producing
countries will ever be resumed in full. The creditors
will have to consent to debt settlements by which
they will forgo a large percentage of their claims.
Thus, anything obtained through the suggested
scheme ought to be regarded as a sheer windfall for
the creditors.

### (4) AN ADDITION TO GOLD RESERVE

Another great advantage of the scheme would be
that it would make it easier for the British authorities to stabilise sterling when the time for stabilisation should come. We do not propose to go into the
details of all the conditions in which it would be
safe to stabilise sterling. For our present purpose, it
is sufficient to point out one. So long as the British

authorities do not possess a gold stock comparable with that of the United States or France, it is not safe to return to the gold standard. The experience of 1925–1931 has shown the disadvantages of attempting to make the gold standard work while Great Britain is in a state of inferiority compared with countries which do not possess a banking centre with the organisation and traditions of London. Unless sterling were technically as strong as the dollar and the franc, the gold standard would be exposed once more to adverse pressure or to shocks through the inexperience and gambling spirit of the United States or through the hoarding habits and political-mindedness of the French. In order to eliminate or at least to mitigate the discrepancy between the British gold reserve on the one hand and the French and American gold reserves on the other, it would be necessary for Great Britain to double and even treble her gold stock. Given the fact that the British balance of payments is barely at equilibrium, it is not easy to visualise this being done for a few years. An increase of the British export surplus is unthinkable amidst the rising tide of economic nationalism all over the world. If the amount of the gold reserve should be increased by a corresponding increase in foreign balances, the technical position of sterling would not be improved. It is unthinkable that this country should obtain in the ordinary course the repayment of its foreign investments on a sufficiently large scale. It is equally unlikely that the British Government will ever consent to issue external loans running into hundreds of millions of pounds for the sake of increasing the permanent gold reserve. While the skilful handling of the Exchange Equalisation Account may result in some further increase in the gold stock, it would take many years before the amount would be large enough for the purpose of restoring the gold standard.

It is thus conceivable that a moment might arrive when all circumstances would favour stabilisation with the exception of the technical strength of sterling. With the aid of our scheme this difficulty could easily be overcome. In his book *The Problems of the Foreign Exchanges*, Mr L. L. B. Angas advocates the substitution of commodity reserves for gold reserves. In this extreme form, this suggestion appears to be impracticable, but there is no reason why gold reserves should not be supplemented by commodity reserves. The possession of £100 million of staple commodities would be equivalent, from the point of view of the technical position of sterling, to the possession of a similar amount of gold. While the possibilities of increasing the gold reserve are limited, there are immense possibilities for acquiring secondary gold reserves in the form of stocks of staple commodities. Thus, from the point of view of the restoration of international monetary stability, the adoption of this scheme would be very helpful.

### (5) ADVANTAGES FOR GREAT BRITAIN

From a purely British point of view, the advantages of the scheme are equally obvious. It would reduce the dependence of Great Britain upon the caprices of international markets. As things are, if for no matter what reason the world market were to cease to buy British goods, the population of Great Britain would be reduced to starvation after the gold reserve had been exhausted. If a blockade of the British Isles were successfully carried out, the population would be on the point of starvation within a few months. The possession of a large food and raw material reserve supply would certainly safeguard this country to a large extent against the worst consequences of a closing of foreign markets to British exports or of a blockade. Needless to say, £100 million worth of food and raw material would not in itself carry us very far, but it would be better than nothing, and once the advantages of the scheme were realised, it is conceivable that the amount would be increased.

Another advantage from a British point of view would be that it would place a powerful bargaining weapon in the hands of the British Government. As things are, Great Britain's dependence upon overseas food and raw material supplies places her at a grave disadvantage, since it is vital for her to import, while it is not nearly so vital for the raw-material-producing countries to purchase British goods. The possession of a strong commodity reserve would place Great Britain in a much better position to obtain advantageous terms in international trade agreements.

We have pointed out above that the adoption of our scheme would make it easier to restore the stability of sterling in given circumstances. The maintenance of the stability of sterling would be equally facilitated. The Government's commodity stocks would play the part of a secondary reserve. In the case of adverse pressure on sterling it would be possible to reduce imports of wheat or raw materials by selling part of the official stocks. This in itself would provide a relief, so that the gold reserve would not have to be drawn upon to an embarrassing degree. If there was buying pressure on sterling, instead of having to

import and sterilise gold which would be missed in
other countries, it would be possible to increase the
Government's commodity reserves.

## (6) OBJECTIONS TO THE SCHEME

Let us now deal with the objections that may possibly be raised against the scheme. The question may
be asked whether foreign debtor countries would be
both able and willing to pay their debts by selling
raw materials to the British Government. As far as
Germany and one or two other industrial debtor
countries are concerned, it would be obviously impossible to apply the scheme. Countries of Latin
America and continental debtor countries such as
Hungary, Roumania, Jugoslavia, etc., are, however,
well in a position to produce a surplus of the kind of
commodities that would be acceptable in payment of
debts. As for their willingness, there can be no doubt
that most of them would be only too pleased to take
the opportunity thus provided for the liquidation of
part of their debts, especially as at the same time the
operation would provide direct assistance to their
producers. In some instances, similar agreements have
actually been concluded. For example, Hungary
settled her accumulated frozen commercial indebtedness to Switzerland in the form of special wheat
exports. As we pointed out above, the attractions of
the scheme from the point of view of the debtor
countries could be increased by an undertaking that
the commodities purchased would not be sold for a
given period. Although the agreement on the details
of such transactions would require lengthy negotiations, there is no reason to suppose that the negotiators

would encounter insurmountable difficulties.

The scheme may be objected to on the ground that it would favour a certain group of creditors at the expense of others. This objection might have carried considerable weight a few years ago, but in the meantime the principle that all creditors are entitled to equal treatment has been discarded on so many occasions that its application is now almost the exception rather than the rule. In any case, other creditor countries are at liberty to follow the British example and accept payment in commodities. Moreover, the unfreezing of part of the credits without a corresponding reduction in the debtors' resources available for debt payment could only be advantageous to the remaining creditors. It would change the ratio between the debtors' assets and liabilities in favour of the creditors.

Another possible objection is that the British purchases might unduly encourage an expansion of the production of staple commodities. There is undoubtedly something in this point, but the same may be said about any influence which leads to an increase in demand and in commodity prices. The Governments of the raw-material-producing countries would fully understand that the transactions in question were essentially not recurrent. It would be for them to prevent their producers from being misled into an undue increase in production. In any case, an amount of £100 million or even twice that figure spread over a large number of countries would hardly do more than liquidate a relatively small part of the surplus stocks. It is not as if it would be necessary to increase actual production in order to satisfy the additional demand.

Another possible objection would be that though it would be all very well while the Government bought commodities, the good effect of its operations would be reversed the moment it began to sell. The importance of this argument should not be exaggerated. If, as there is every reason to hope, the application of the scheme were followed by a revival of trade, the movement, once it had been set in motion, would not be halted even by the complete liquidation of the stocks originally acquired.

### (7) OPPOSITION TO GOVERNMENT INTERVENTION

There remain the conventional objections against Government intervention in economic life and the usual arguments against the inefficiency of Governments in business. We do not propose to examine here the whole controversy of *laissez-faire* versus intervention. It is sufficient to point out that the trend of evolution is decidedly in favour of increased Government intervention, and the adoption of the scheme would be in keeping with this trend. Finally, it may be argued that the possession of commodities by the Government might entail financial losses. Even if that were the case, the advantages of the scheme would make it worth while to put up with losses, especially since the amount used would represent an unearned profit on the revaluation of the gold reserve. There is, however, no reason to suppose that there would be any material losses; in fact, on balance the probability is that the Government would make a profit, since it would be initiating an upward movement in commodity prices. This is, however, a purely secondary consideration, just as the profit or loss on the operations of the Exchange Equalisation Account is a matter of secondary importance.

The author does not claim that the scheme is watertight in all its details. Once the fundamental principle has been approved, the details can be elaborated by those possessing expert knowledge of commodity markets, and of the requirements of this country in non-perishable commodities, etc. It should be comparatively easy to find a formula by which the profit on the gold reserve could be mobilised before it was definitely fixed through the legal stabilisation of sterling.

To conclude, the author has to point out that he does not altogether claim the merit of originality for his proposals. Apart from the idea put forward by Major Angas which was referred to above, there have been precedents in the past for prominent Governments accumulating commodity stocks for rainy days. The first of these precedents dates back to 4000 B.C. or thereabouts. It was adopted in Egypt on the suggestion of an economic expert named Joseph, thanks to whom Egypt was in a position to face with equanimity the seven lean years.

THE END